SCHOLASTIC

TRANSFORMING LITERACY TEACHING

IN THE ERA OF HIGHER STANDARDS

Midge Madden & Valarie Lee

New York · Toronto · London · Auckland · Sydney
Mexico City · New Delhi · Hong Kong · Buenos Aires

Acknowledgment

A special thank you to Mary Byatt, Tia Cade, Kathy Carhart, Chad Cooper, Kara Damminger, Robin DeGarmo, Donna McGough, Amy Pridgen, and Dave Raudenbush for your invaluable contributions to this book. Thank you for your willingness to open your classrooms and to try out new approaches so that we could learn beside you.

Cover Designer: Jorge J. Namerow
Interior Designer: Sydney Wright

ISBN: 978-0-545-61251-7
Copyright © 2015 by Midge Madden and Valarie Lee
All rights reserved.
Published by Scholastic Inc.
Printed in the U.S.A.

1 2 3 4 5 6 7 8 9 10   40   22 21 20 19 18 17 16 15

Contents

Introduction

> "It is state and local leaders and teachers themselves who, ultimately, must make the Standards into an effective instructional reality—what happens day to day in classrooms determines student ELA learning."
>
> —International Reading Association

The school library had emptied out, except for a few middle school teachers who sat hunched over copies of the Common Core State Standards, handouts on the Danielson evaluation system, and sample PARCC questions.

"I don't get it," lamented Gerry, shaking her head in visible frustration. "We have these all-day-long professional development sessions that are supposed to help us but instead only give us more to stress about! Teaching middle schoolers is challenging enough without this perfect storm of new standards, new teacher evaluations, and new assessments."

"Amen to that," echoed Brad. "I am still trying to figure out how to implement the Common Core in my daily lessons. That's what I need help with! I teach history and science. Now I'm supposed to teach reading, too?"

"Yeah." Cheryl agreed. She waved her hand over the stack of Danielson handouts. "And how can we be evaluated on something we're just learning to do? All these instructional shifts everyone is talking about—more nonfiction, close readings of complex texts, short research-based inquiry projects—how will this impact our curriculums? Or will those change as well?"

Jeremy leaned back in his chair, wearing a thoughtful look on his face. "You know," he began, "I've been around a lot of years and have weathered many top-down directives, but this Common Core thing—this is somehow different, and I think it's here to stay. There's something to this twenty-first-century thing. Schools are going to have to change if we want to keep up with this rapidly changing world. Think about our students. Few are truly interested in school. Ask what gets them excited and most will talk about out-of-school activities like texting and social media stuff. I think the bigger question is how can we win our kids back. The Common Core just may give us the opportunity to do that."

"Hmmm, maybe," Cheryl nodded. But I still get angry! Principals and supervisors don't even know how to implement the standards, and they're going to assess us? I refuse to teach to the test. I'm sorry, but it seems like the state and federal government march in and lay it all out, and we're expected to just march to their drum."

"So, how do we counter that?" responded Brad. "How do we regain control over our classrooms and kids?"

These teachers aren't alone—much confusion and misinterpretation about the current standards abound. We hear this echoed in our work with teachers in schools and candidates in our graduate programs. And, as more and more teachers receive training on the standards, conflicting messages threaten to undermine the standards' transformational potential.

Perhaps if we consider a portrait of the college-and-career ready student, teachers and administrators might more easily understand that the standards are not a curriculum or a checklist but rather guiding, overarching goals that students need to master in order to be successful in college and in life. Looking specifically at the goals of the new English Language Arts standards, students will become increasingly competent in reading, writing, speaking, listening, and language as they progress through the grades. And they will increasingly exhibit key characteristics of the college-and-career ready person—someone who is able to:

- work independently

- access a strong base of content knowledge

- respond to the varying demands of audience, task, purpose, and discipline

- comprehend as well as critique

- understand the value of evidence

- use technology and digital media strategically and capably

- understand other perspectives and cultures

(CCSS Initiative, 2014)

So, keeping in mind the ultimate goal of college-and-career ready individuals, how can we use the English Language Arts standards as road maps to help all students become college and career ready? What do we need to understand in order to effectively implement the standards in our everyday teaching and learning in today's classrooms? How must our beliefs about teaching and learning change?

Instructional Shifts for English Language Arts

The new standards in English Language Arts require three major instructional shifts:

- regular practice with complex text and its academic language

- building knowledge through content-rich nonfiction

- reading, writing, and speaking grounded in evidence from both literary and informational text

The goal of these shifts in ELA is to help students meet the demands of college and career literacy. The following paragraphs highlight key points about each shift.

REGULAR PRACTICE WITH COMPLEX TEXT AND ITS ACADEMIC LANGUAGE

Teachers hear much about the importance of students gaining independence in reading complex texts: "To grow, our students must read lots, and more specifically they must read lots of 'complex' texts—texts that offer them new language, new knowledge, and new modes of thought" (Adams, 2009, p. 182). Yet, many teachers interpret this to mean that building independence comes at the expense of students struggling with text without support, leaving them to tackle difficult texts alone.

The standards for grades 6–12 in history/social studies, science, and technical subjects incorporate the instructional shifts in ELA.

Transforming Literacy Teaching in the Era of Higher Standards © 2015 by Midge Madden and Valarie Lee, Scholastic Teaching Resources

The new standards aim to discover what it takes for students to learn, sometimes through deep involvement by the teacher, sometimes not. "For many, challenging text is the right ground to maximize learning . . . but the only way that using such challenging text will work is if students get substantial teaching support in the context of that hard text" (Shanahan, 2011).

BUILDING KNOWLEDGE THROUGH CONTENT-RICH NONFICTION

Besides using complex texts, the standards also emphasize the importance of integrating more nonfiction into all content areas including English Language Arts. Although there is (and perhaps needs to be) more emphasis on teaching informational texts with the standards, a balance between using informational and narrative texts is essential. We can teach students that there is a need for both in a reader's world in all disciplines. Poetry, dramatic readings, and reader response to literature coupled with nonfiction content engage students. Students should be allowed to feel and respond emotionally and aesthetically to texts as well as simply comprehend the facts at the efferent level.

READING, WRITING, AND SPEAKING GROUNDED IN EVIDENCE FROM BOTH LITERARY AND INFORMATIONAL TEXT

Whether students are reading or writing, speaking or listening, the standards call upon them to use evidence from text to support their thinking. The emphasis on evidence across multiple literacies allows students to fully develop their use of evidence from text. For example, when listening to a speaker arguing for more environmental protections, students must be able to discern the speaker's claim and the evidence used to support that claim. When reading a narrative, students must draw evidence from the descriptions to make an inference about a character's motivation.

But to make the goals of these English Language Arts shifts achievable, we must also remember to keep the individual students at the center of our instruction.

Students at the Core

In order to reach the ultimate goal of the standards—producing college-and-career ready literate individuals—we argue that our traditional notions of teaching and learning must change.

Instead of viewing the standards as the core of what we do, we need to place our students in the center. The standards' profile of a high school graduate is centered on the graduate, the learner, the student.

Yet, how do teachers striving to enact the standards keep the student at the center? Standards call for more independence, but how do teachers interpret independence? A student-centered pedagogy acknowledges student voice as central to the learning experience for every learner and requires students to be active, responsible participants in their own learning. Students work in flexible, cooperative groupings to solve problems and analyze texts to demonstrate understanding of a task or concept through multiple perspectives. Work is mostly rigorous. Students can articulate the how and why of their learning.

> "We've forgotten a basic premise of education: The learner does the learning. If we're doing the work, then they're not doing the learning. The Common Core can be an opportunity to shift the work of learning from our own backs onto the shoulders of our students, where it belongs."
>
> —Laura Thomas (2013)

Edutopia, the Buck Institute for Education, and Coalition for Essential Schools provide excellent resources for student-centered inquiry and project-based learning. As teachers experiment with new ways to engage and give more responsibility to their students, they need time to meet, talk, and collaborate with one another. Reflective practice becomes embedded in day-to-day decisions and supports teachers as they navigate the new standards and grapple with their implications for practice.

Centering teaching on the learner and not the curriculum represents a major change in thinking for many teachers, both new and experienced. While some teachers may have already realized that engagement and motivation to learn increase when students have autonomy, choice, and independence, these ideas may be new to other teachers. A major purpose of this book is to help teachers understand the potential of a student-centered pedagogy as well as show ways that they can adapt traditional teacher-directed instruction to better engage and motivate students, and ultimately teach more effectively to meet higher standards. The following section describes a framework for developing student-centered lessons that we hope is helpful as teachers begin to rethink their practice.

A Framework for Developing Student-Centered Lessons

We have created a framework through which to read and understand the lessons presented in the following chapters of this book. As you study our framework in the figure below, read the corresponding descriptions of each component that explain the expectations required of teachers and students in student-centered classrooms. Then refer to the Reflective Questions resource (see the Online Resources section, page 16), keeping in mind the framework, as you create your own lessons that put students at the core.

Knowledge Production | Engagement

STUDENTS AT THE CORE

Voice | Independence

KNOWLEDGE PRODUCTION

Students approach a problem and inquire about it by addressing open-ended, essential questions. Students learn to produce knowledge through the deep reading and rereading of text and share their knowledge with a larger audience. Emphasis is placed on learning to learn and the belief that people become smarter through reading texts. Teachers in student-centered classrooms create tasks that integrate reading, writing, speaking, and listening.

As you plan your lessons, ask yourself:

- Do students have opportunities to develop their own questions about text?

- Do my questions include open-ended, essential questions?

- Do students use inquiry practices to research and develop content knowledge?

- Do students use multiple readings of the text to learn content?

ENGAGEMENT

A 21st-century classroom capitalizes on technology to enhance learning and amplify student work to reach a larger audience. Interactive tasks and interesting, authentic texts worthy of deep reading have the potential to help students reach the rigorous goals set forth by the Common Core.

As you plan your lessons, ask yourself:

- What in the lesson addresses students' interests?

- What kinds of digital tools could be used to engage students in meaningful literacy tasks?

- Could one of my more traditional practices reach larger audiences? Could it be amplified by replacing it with a digital tool?

Transforming Literacy Teaching in the Era of Higher Standards © 2015 by Midge Madden and Valarie Lee, Scholastic Teaching Resources

INDEPENDENCE

In the move from teacher-directed to student-centered classrooms, students take on the task of learning while skillful teachers know when and where to scaffold learning. Strategic use of scaffolding allows teachers to modify instruction based on individual student needs, rather than as an immediate support for everyone, allowing students to meet higher expectations.

As you plan your lessons, ask yourself:

- Are the activities presented in a way to challenge students sufficiently?

- Are students ready to take on more of the task independently?

- Have I planned scaffolding and frontloading purposefully?

VOICE

Increased student talk and ownership of classroom discussions have the potential to transform learning. In addition, the motivation and engagement of students occurs when classroom activities and decisions begin with student choice and control. Teachers in student-centered classrooms facilitate learning, use flexible groups, and give students meaningful feedback on their progress.

As you plan your lessons, ask yourself:

- Have I provided multiple opportunities for student talk?

- Do students have sufficient time to discuss ideas and text deeply?

- Have I planned for authentic discussions rather than teacher question/student response?

- Do students have control and choice in the lesson?

- How do I gather and provide meaningful feedback for students while listening in to student conversations?

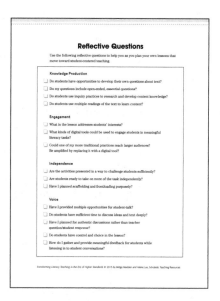

Reflective Questions—downloadable pdf available online (see page 16)

In order to fully understand our framework, we must define what we mean by "teaching moves." The Common Core State Standards have the potential to change teaching and learning by providing focus on teaching moves, or teaching decisions, that place students at the center. What modifications can we make in our practice to better meet individual needs yet also meet higher standards? It is commonly agreed that if today's classrooms are to support students as they strive for college and career readiness, teaching and learning in these classrooms must look very different.

Teachers are currently being inundated with examples of model Common Core lessons, but how do they use them to transform their current practice and get to the next level? Changing the ways teaching and learning looks in schools is not a simple undertaking. The standards can provide guidance, but the work of changing instruction and reshaping curriculums must be done by teachers and administrators. In so doing, educators must be mindful that teaching and curriculums are, of necessity, fluid and subject to change in response to needs of the students.

How This Book Is Organized

We acknowledge that teaching today demands much of teachers, so we offer this book as a resource to help teachers make these changes in their instruction. We feature real teachers, students, and classroom scenarios. We set out to discover what teachers really experience as they try to navigate the standards and implement them effectively in their middle school classrooms.

Our book focuses on putting students at the core and addressing the new and higher standards through student motivation and engagement. We also address the major instructional shifts that implementing the English Language Arts standards require of middle school teachers and we present lessons in which the ELA CCSS strands (reading, writing, speaking and listening, and language) for middle school grades are addressed, including several that integrate reading and social studies.

It is not our intent that the lessons included here represent the full spectrum of pedagogical practices and teaching moves necessary to integrate all standards; instead, we hope they will spark collegial conversations and personal reflection on creating more student-centered classrooms as teachers integrate new practices into their classrooms.

 Transforming Literacy Teaching in the Era of Higher Standards © 2015 by Midge Madden and Valarie Lee, Scholastic Teaching Resources

In each chapter, we examine a specific English Language Arts area. Each chapter opens with a discussion of the particular teaching focus and then presents sets of teacher-directed lessons and student-centered lessons. We first provide a lesson that represents a teacher-directed approach to addressing specific standards. We reflect on what parts of the lesson address the standards and what is missing, then provide a second lesson that illustrates a more student-centered approach to teaching the same standards. A side-by-side analysis of the two lessons, taking into account the four elements of our framework, provides insights into the teaching moves used to transition from traditional teacher-directed lessons to more student-centered lessons. Although we argue as authors and teachers for a student-centered focus in our practice, we don't suggest that direct instruction is never necessary. We do believe that a student-centered approach can transform "good" traditional, teacher-directed instruction to "great" inspired teaching that will ultimately produce fully literate young people who are college and career prepared.

> Teachers and curriculum developers must lead implementation of the standards, and they need administrative support and district autonomy in order to do so well. It is imperative that all educators receive the time necessary to get the standards right and make them work in schools. This underscores the importance of teachers' voices in decisions about implementation of the standards.

In Chapter 1, we focus on reading, specifically the reading of informational text. The six lessons featured in this chapter provide examples for integrating the literacy standards in language arts and social studies.

Chapter 2 presents four lessons that focus on the speaking and listening standards for middle school grades. The lessons address the importance of recognizing varying levels of student talk and allowing student control of classroom discussions centered on young adult literature.

Chapter 3 includes lessons integrating the standards for writing. These four lessons highlight ways that students can learn to write strong argument essays and more fully comprehend historical events through dramatization.

Chapter 4 spotlights four lessons emphasizing the importance of planning for inquiry and using technology as a collaborative tool to extend students' work to larger audiences.

In Chapter 5, we present a look at the integrated nature of the Common Core standards as a middle school teacher narrates and reflects on the use of dramatizations in her literature unit. We address ways to re-envision teaching and learning in the 21st century and look at the potential for the standards to meet those challenges. We also reflect on Common Core teaching and the synergy currently building across schools, districts, and states as teachers more deeply invest in a re-conceptualized reality of what it means to learn and to know.

Online Resources

There are companion resources available online. To access this material, go to **teacherexpress.scholastic.com/transforming-literacy-teaching-middleschool**. There you will be able to view videos that will enhance your understanding of this book's material, and find other helpful teacher resources. You will also be able to download the following ready-to-use student resources:

- 5Ws Graphic Organizer

- Primary Sources Analysis Sheet

- Annotation Bookmark

- K-W-L Chart

- Inquiry Chart

- Dramatizing History Planning Sheet

- Digital Citizenship Guidelines

Once downloaded, the student resources may be distributed to students to use individually or in small groups. You may also display a pdf version on an interactive whiteboard for whole-class learning. These resources, while mentioned specifically in the model lessons, are easily adaptable to many lessons and topics you teach.

Chapter 1

Reading Authentic Informational Text

> "Teachers need to establish an ambitious itinerary of rich and varied narrative and informational texts, including some texts that are easier than the Standards specify.
>
> "Athletes vary their routines to build strength, flexibility, and stamina; likewise, readers need reading experiences with a range of text difficulties and lengths if they are to develop these characteristics as readers."
>
> —International Reading Association

Common Core teaching engages students in the reading of text at multiple levels of difficulty; however, the shift in the standards rests in the reading of rigorous, complex text. Based on the ACT 2006 Reading Between the Lines study finding that the ability to read complex text is a strong predictor of college success, the standards require regular reading of rigorous text. But how much complex text should be read and how teachers should support students in their reading remains to be answered.

Timothy Shanahan (2012) uses the analogy of a bicycle to describe the teacher's role. Overuse of scaffolds without increasing the challenge of the task results in students' reliance on training wheels to complete the task. He calls upon teachers to become, instead, the "helmet, protecting students from harm as they stretch their reading skills and stamina through teacher-supported instruction of complex text." Furthermore, the International Reading Association specifies:

> The CCSS guidelines on text complexity encourage teachers to engage students in reading at least some texts they are likely to struggle with in terms of fluency and reading comprehension. This represents a major shift in instructional approach. To ensure that the interactions with such texts lead to maximum student learning, teachers must provide significantly greater and more skillful instructional scaffolding—employing rereading, explanation, encouragement, and other supports within lessons. (p. 1)

This kind of reading is often framed as allowing students to "productively struggle" with complex text under the careful guidance of the teacher. Fisher and Frey (2012) maintain that:

> With appropriately scaffolded instruction that is indeed based on continuous teacher assessment of the increasing bank of knowledge and language that a student has on a topic being studied, a student can learn to read texts that are beyond his or her instructional level and hopefully learn how to support his or her own reading. (p. 7)

Common Core teaching also emphasizes reading texts across disciplinary fields such as science and social studies. Although the standards document provides teachers in grades 6–12 with a separate section of reading standards for disciplinary text, fifth grade teachers will find these standards integrated in the K–5 reading standards.

Clearly, emphasis must be on *appropriate* scaffolds. In some cases, this means turning over the reading task to students without extensive frontloading; in other

Transforming Literacy Teaching in the Era of Higher Standards © 2015 by Midge Madden and Valarie Lee, Scholastic Teaching Resources

cases, pre-teaching vocabulary and activating schema are appropriate to help students increase their reading skills and stamina.

Although the standards document does not specifically refer to close reading, careful, purposeful rereading is supported.

In this chapter, the six model lessons in action focus on close reading, introducing complex text, and integrating reading standards in social studies. In presenting the lessons, we follow six middle school classroom teachers as they engage students in learning and reading about the Civil War through the use of primary documents and secondary accounts.

Asking Their Own Questions: What Can Students Discover?

The first lesson, Reading Multiple Texts, is a teacher-directed lesson. The second lesson, Jigsaw of Multiple Primary Documents, incorporates key instructional shifts such as regular practice with complex text and building knowledge through content-rich nonfiction.

Teacher-Directed Lesson: Reading Multiple Texts

Ms. McGough's classroom is inviting, and rich in print and technology. Students sit in four-person pods. Yesterday they learned about the firing on Fort Sumter, and Ms. M is reviewing the events with them now. She informs them that they will be learning about the first battle of the Civil War and reminds them about their essential questions:

- What divides a nation?

- What is the human side of war?

For the next five minutes, Ms. M reviews important facts about the beginning of the Civil War, focusing on events leading up to the first Battle of Bull Run, the event students will be studying today. Ms. M asks, "Why were people in the North mad about the lack of battles?"

Melinda: They had soldiers and the soldiers weren't fighting.

Jason: And they only signed up for 90 days! Time's almost up!

"Great thinking! Now you are going to read an overview of the battle out of your textbook. As you read these two pages, remember to use your reading guide." The students pull out their copy of a graphic organizer that has been designed to guide them in answering questions about an event using the 5Ws: who, what, where, when, and why.

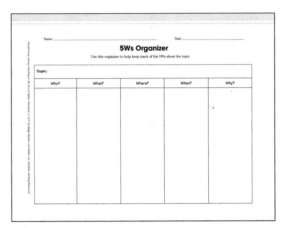

5Ws graphic organizer—downloadable pdf is available online (see page 16)

Ms. M prepares them further. "This battle has a lot of significant events, which you are going to read about. Later, you will write in your journal. So, if you find anything interesting, add it to your organizer." Students begin immediately, reading quietly and noting facts on their organizers.

After about 15 minutes, Ms. M has students share facts they noted.

Charise: They actually came with picnic lunches.
Important people came to the battlefield.

Max: Isn't that stupid? Wouldn't they get shot?

When Amanda notes that the map they read in the text put the battle between Richmond and Washington, D.C., at Manassa Junction, Ms. M opens the floor to student discussion, asking, "Why is the location significant? Talk about it with those at your table." A spirited discussion commences at nearly every table. Most students correctly identify that the battle is between the two capitals. Ms. M draws their attention to the map projected with the document reader and defines a "junction" as an important transportation center for troops and supplies. She then clicks on a link to show students a video clip from Ken Burns' Civil War documentary. As students watch, they add more information to their reading guides.

"Tomorrow, I want to show you letters from an actual soldier who fought for the Union in the infantry. He fought in the Battle of Bull Run, and through my research, I found his actual letters. But do you know what is really amazing?" asks Ms. M.

She pauses, and students look on in anticipation. She continues, "He lived in Woodbury, not that far from our school!" This piques the students' interest. Francine asks, "So, are the letters actually real?" Sam looks at his table partner and exclaims, "Wow! Cool!"

Teacher Reflection

"What I see is engagement and bolstered student confidence. There is a link between what we are doing with primary documents and close reading, and they are starting to stretch themselves and challenge themselves. Plus, more and more of my students are choosing to read nonfiction. The librarian told me, 'Your kids are taking all my nonfiction!' When they finish a book, they often suggest, 'Maybe someone will want to read this,' and place it on my windowsill. The kids are seeing that there are other types of reading."

—Donna McGough

✔ HOW DOES THE LESSON MEET THE STANDARDS?

Students are encouraged to make inferences from multiple text sources, such as secondary texts, visuals, graphics, and video. Students must also listen in order to extract information from a video. Student engagement during the lesson is high, with most students expressing interest in some aspect of the lesson. Partner and small-group conversations indicate that students are focused on the evidence from the text. Students' questions, especially the non-prompted ones, indicate higher-order thinking, often anticipating a question before the teacher has asked it. Through her questioning, Ms. M pushes her students to think more deeply about historical events and their implications.

WHAT'S MISSING?

The text students read is easy for most of Ms. M's students, with the exception of some struggling readers. Furthermore, much of the information about the battle is built through teacher explanation or whole-class discussions rather than engaging students in reading and discussions. While small-group and partner talk occurs, the discussion is still more centered on a teacher-prompted question instead of an open-ended prompt that requires students to collaborate in order to create knowledge. Luckily, because of the work Ms. M has already done in her classroom, students would be able to handle open-ended prompts independently.

PLACING STUDENTS AT THE CORE OF A STANDARDS-BASED LESSON

As you read the next lesson, consider how this teacher, Ms. Denton, does the following:

- uses the jigsaw strategy and technology to position students to take more control of the discussion

- increases the rigor of text by providing primary documents

- scaffolds for students' comprehension challenges by providing texts at different levels

- positions students to produce historical knowledge through careful reading of text rather than simply engaging in whole-class discussions and showing a video

Student-Centered Lesson: Jigsaw of Multiple Primary Documents

Students in Ms. Denton's classroom sit in three mixed-ability groups. Ms. D reveals the lesson's essential questions on the interactive whiteboard:

- What was significant about the first battle of the Civil War?

- What is the human side of war?

Students then view a large color map of the battlefield and surrounding areas on the interactive whiteboard. Ms. D continues, "We need to figure out why a map would be important to look at and what might be significant about where this battle is taking place." She gives students a minute to discuss in their groups, and in the meantime pulls up a primary sources graphic organizer with five blocks labeled "Map," "Photograph," "Walt Whitman," "Confederate Soldier," and "Newspaper Editor." She calls the class together and points to the first block titled "Map." Students share their responses about the map's importance, which Ms. D records on the interactive organizer. "This is where we are going to keep our notes as we learn more and more about this battle. When we are done, you will be able to answer our essential questions," which she reads aloud.

Primary Sources Analysis Sheet— downloadable pdf is available online (see page 16)

Next, a black and white photograph of citizens of Washington, D.C., on a hill overlooking the battlefield flashes on the interactive whiteboard. Ms. D poses the question, "What do you notice about the picture?" Students in her classroom are familiar with "reading" photographs; as Ms. D has taught them how to break the picture into four quadrants to look for details. Students study the photograph carefully, and lively conversations ensue. Ms. D directs them to add their responses to the section of the organizer titled "Photograph."

Samantha: They are dressed up. The men are wearing ties and coats.

Brock: There's fancy dishes on the ground. Seems weird. Why would they bring dishes to a battle?

Madison: It's like a picnic . . . at a fight!

Bree: Ms. Denton, what if someone already wrote up there what we wanted to add?

Salvatore: We could just put a plus next to it to say we agree!

Ms. D: Great idea, Salvatore. Keep going!

Encouraging students to go deeper as they continue to focus on the two essential questions, Ms. D now forms new groups of three, this time grouping by similar reading level. She distributes a primary document to each group (a journal entry from Walt Whitman; a letter from a soldier; or a newspaper article) matching the difficulty level of the document to her students' reading abilities.

She asks, "What can you infer about the attitude of the particular citizen toward this first battle? First, you will work independently. Read and study the primary document carefully and record what you find. Use what you have learned about taking notes and jot down right on your document. Later, you will compare your findings with those of others in your group."

Students annotate their primary documents, marking any information that will help them answer the questions. Ms. D reminds them to use the online dictionary if context clues don't help them define difficult vocabulary. She monitors their progress as she walks around and reads their annotations. Once they're done, each groups' task is to discuss what they annotated individually and summarize their analysis of the document on the interactive graphic organizer. Ms. D conferences with each group to ascertain any difficulty they had comprehending and analyzing the document. She encourages each group to reread as needed and pay careful attention to the language the writer uses.

After ten minutes, Ms. D mixes the students to create groups whose three members each represent one of the documents. In these mixed groups, each student, or "expert," teaches his or her document to the other two members, using the comments posted on the whiteboard interactive organizer as a guide.

To close the lesson, Ms. D ends by collecting unanswered questions from students. "Everyone, what do you still want to know about the battle? What hasn't been answered through the reading of these documents? Would you please write these below our chart so we can come back to them tomorrow? Also, what resources might we use to answer them?" Some students record their questions:

Mark: How many soldiers died in the battle?

Andrea: What happened afterwards?

Sam: Did people who wanted the war so bad feel bad after?

"An excellent start, everyone. Keep thinking of those questions that puzzle you. We can add to the list throughout the day if you remember more."

Side-by-Side Lesson Analysis

Framework Element	Reading Multiple Texts	➤ Teaching Moves ➤	Jigsaw of Multiple Primary Documents
Knowledge Production	Teacher gives information about the battle through explanations and use of a secondary text source.	Reduce frontloading background information in order to allow a space for students themselves to generate knowledge about the battle. Include scaffolds, such as starting with visuals as models for analysis before moving to print.	Students synthesize multiple primary documents to analyze important events of the battle using jigsaw strategy to build knowledge.
Engagement	Students read text, but display interest to go beyond the text. Students display interest in the multiple texts provided, but are especially interested in the prospect of reading firsthand accounts.	Use authentic, primary documents, only bringing in textbook as a way to scaffold struggling readers and as a quick resource to answer questions not answered by the primary documents.	Students use technology (interactive graphic organizer on whiteboard) to record their analysis. Students read primary accounts of the battle, rich in vivid descriptions of the actions and emotions of the day.
Independence	Students experience little difficulty reading about the Battle of Bull Run in a secondary text. All students read the same textbook pages on Bull Run.	Give control of the discussion to student groups while facilitating and clarifying confusion.	Students read primary sources of varying degrees of difficulty, allowing all students to experience appropriately rigorous text.
Voice	Classroom discussions mostly center on teacher-question/student-response format. Some small-group discussions center on more open-ended questions.	Provide open-ended questions for every student to consider. Encourage student-created questions. Put each student in the role of "expert" on their document.	Students use their reading to investigate open-ended questions and present these findings during jigsaw group discussions.

Building Independence:
Are Students Ready to Take It On?

The first lesson, Reading Comprehension of Social Studies Textbook, is a teacher-directed lesson. The second lesson, Close Reading of Primary Document incorporates key instructional shifts such as reading, writing, and speaking grounded in evidence from both literary and informational text, knowledge production through content-rich nonfiction, and regular practice with complex text and its academic language.

Teacher-Directed Lesson:
Reading Comprehension of Social Studies Textbook

Mr. Meyers is attempting to bring his class of energetic middle schoolers together for social studies after finishing the language arts block. "OK, everyone, let's get those social studies books out quickly! I want to start by telling you that we are going to read about a really interesting group of people in the Civil War." He displays the word *abolitionists* on the interactive whiteboard.

"We are going to use this graphic organizer as a way to keep track of the things we learn about the abolitionists." Mr. M models the K-W-L chart using the document camera.

He continues, "An abolitionist is a person who was really important during the Civil War. I want you to write in the first block of your organizer under 'What I Know' anything you know about abolitionists and what they did during the Civil War." After one minute, he asks students to turn and talk with a partner, to share what they know.

Nancy: I think I've heard about them somewhere.

Michael: Weren't they in that last chapter?

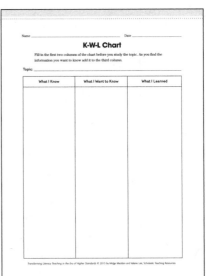

K-W-L Chart—downloadable pdf is available online (see page 16)

After listening to exchanges like this one and asking the students to share their responses with the whole group, it is apparent that they know little about the abolitionists, except maybe for Chad, who replied, "They were a group people that didn't like slavery and wanted to get rid of it."

Mr. M reassures students, saying, "It's OK that we don't know a lot about them because we are going to read about them today in our text. So let's write, 'What are abolitionists?' in the second box, 'What I Want to Know.' To get you ready, I'll give you a little background. We're going to watch a five-minute clip from a movie, and I want you to record any new things you learn in the third box of your organizer under 'What I Learned.'" The lights dim as he plays a video about abolitionists from the History Channel. Students watch the video with interest and fill in the graphic organizer with names and events.

After the students share new facts that they discovered, Mr. M brings up a slide show he created to give students more background. He spends about four minutes showing them pictures of famous abolitionists and key events during the war. Students also see pictures of primary documents, such as the front page of the abolitionist paper, *The Liberator*. Mr. M stops periodically and asks students to jot down more notes in the "What I Know" column.

Then he continues, "Now that we have a lot of background, let's take a look at our textbooks to learn more. As I read out loud, pay attention to new facts, events, and people that influence the abolition movement. I will stop periodically so we can discuss and ask questions."

The students follow along in their textbook as Mr. M reads the two-page account. He stops at several points, asking questions and encouraging the students to ask questions as well. Sarah asks if she can read the rest out loud, and he says yes. As it is nearly time for lunch dismissal, Mr. M closes the lesson by asking students if they have any questions that have not been answered. He has them add these to the middle column, "What I Want to Know," and then collects students' graphic organizers. "I'll take a look at what you wrote down, and we'll discuss the reading more tomorrow. Good work, everybody!"

HOW DOES THE LESSON MEET THE STANDARDS?

What is clear from Mr. M's lesson is that he engages students and builds schema through using multiple resources. He also uses technology effectively to provide rich details about the abolitionists. Because many of his students struggle when reading their middle school social studies text, Mr. M provides multiple scaffolds and strategies to guide their comprehension:

- graphic organizer to write notes

- video clip and slide show to provide background knowledge

- teacher read-aloud

While much confusion exists about the role of frontloading, or pre-teaching, in the new standards, knowing when to frontload and when to let students work with the text first is an important teaching move.

 WHAT'S MISSING?

Because Mr. M activates and builds background knowledge extensively in the lesson, little time is left for students to build knowledge through reading. What's more, he takes on the reading task for students, using the read-aloud to scaffold their comprehension. In order for students to build stamina in reading and reach rigorous reading levels, students need opportunities to struggle productively with complex text.

PLACING STUDENTS AT THE CORE OF A STANDARDS-BASED LESSON

As you read the next lesson taught by Ms. Cade, consider how she:

- turns more of the reading task over to students

- engages all students, including her special needs students, in academic talk

- builds independent reading skills through close reading of text

- uses authentic text to engage her students and move beyond the textbook

Student-Centered Lesson:
Close Reading of Primary Document

Ms. Cade's middle school classroom is alive with student talk as her students view and discuss a photograph from an 1800s cotton plantation on the interactive whiteboard. Students point out important details while examining each of the quadrants of the photograph. She reminds them that their goal is to go deeper into the photograph, asking, "What do you notice the second time?"

Adam blurts out, "What I noticed in the picture is that little girl is expected to carry a basket bigger than her. I wouldn't be able to carry it!"

Ms. C smiles. "You're absolutely right, Adam. Let's find out some more. Go back to the excerpt from George Fitzhugh's *Slaves Without Masters* that we read yesterday. Look at the notes you recorded on that primary document." Students refer to their notes to remember what they noticed. After turning and talking, students share:

Joshua: Well, they are not the happiest.
They were slaves, after all.

Melinda: Yeah, but Fitzhugh made it seem great to be a slave . . .

Sam: Who said that? Just because they sang songs? Does that mean slaves were happy? I think technically they are not happy at all. In music class we learned about slave songs like "Chariots of Heaven," and they are all about being free.

Ms. C: So, what do you think about the article? Believable?

Frank: It's a big lie. How can you be free when you are locked up?

Ms. C: Whose point of view is it?

Juanita: It must be Fitzhugh's. He's trying to make the South look good. I bet he's from the South and maybe even a slave owner.

Frank: Yeah, he's trying to say the South is the best place in the world. You know, trying to brag a little that the South is better.

"Good thinking, everyone," Ms. C remarks as she transitions into the purpose of the day's text reading: to closely read a speech and determine the point of view. She provides a brief context without identifying the speaker as Frederick Douglass. "Our primary document today is a part of a speech that was given about the 4th of July in the 1800s." To activate students' schema, she asks students to turn and talk about a 4th of July celebration they remember. She does this quickly, allowing no more than a minute. She focuses students' attention on an essential question:

- What kinds of things would a speaker say in a 4th of July speech?

Mariella: Maybe give a history of what happened that day? To kind of tell why it is such a special day?

Samson: The person would mention the Declaration of Independence, for sure. He'd probably say that 150 years ago today our nation was formed and the course of our history would not be without that document.

Zach: He'd also talk about freedom, I think.

"Excellent points." Ms. C nods in agreement. Then she hands out a copy of Frederick Douglass' "The Meaning of 4th of July for the Negro" speech. She has provided students with vocabulary definitions on the side of the page and has adapted the speech to shorten the length and create divisions between sections. Students also have an annotation bookmark to remind them how to annotate in the margin space. It is clear, however, that most students have internalized this reading strategy and do not need to refer to the bookmark.

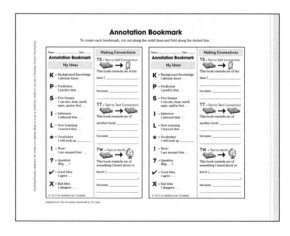

Annotation Bookmark—downloadable pdf is available online (see page 16)

Ms. C explains, "I am not going to tell you who wrote the speech or the exact year it was written. Right now, I want you to choose a discussion partner. Once you have a partner and a bookmark, find a desk. Take a minute to get settled, then you can read and discuss the speech."

Before beginning the task, she reminds students that when they discuss, they need to comment on each other's ideas instead of just reading their comments. She also reminds them that they can reread while waiting for their partners to finish a section. The students immediately begin reading and annotating in the text. Sammy, who struggles with comprehension, puts in earbuds and, with the help of Ms. Sanchez, the instructional aide, starts listening to a recording of Ms. C reading the speech while following along with the printed speech. His partner, Manny, reads silently next to him.

Ms. C quietly monitors the students, reading over their shoulders, and noting student progress on her assessment chart clipboard with notes, such as:

- *Robert needs help annotating within each section.*

- *Amir writes that it seems ironic that the writer is talking about lack of freedom in a 4th of July speech.*

- *Latisha's annotations indicate that she is experiencing difficulty with first two sections: "Why sad? Death? Mourning? Did something happen? Why is it hideous?"*

After a few minutes, quiet partner discussion is heard across the classroom. The conversations are on track and self-monitored by the students. Partners engage in these discussions independently without the need for redirecting interruptions. In fact, students read, discuss, reread, and discuss for 20 minutes, with most students getting through four sections of the speech. Ms. C facilitates with short conferences and sits beside partners to assess, but students control their talk. She asks questions, pushing students to dig deeper:

- What makes you think . . .?

- Where do you find some support for . . .?

She visits Latisha and her partner to check in on the confusion she'd observed earlier. She notices that in sections three and four of the document, Latisha is beginning to gain more comprehension, supported by her partner's comments.

Ms. C then directs the students to join another pair to form a quad. Students are to continue discussing the speech, looking for the speaker's point of view and evidence of who this speaker might be. She prompts them:

- Think of one thing you can share and provide text support for it.

Groups form, and talk happens quickly. Students lean toward one another, nodding in agreement or simply listening.

> Amir: Whoever this is, he did what I thought he would in the first section. But then he talks like he is not happy.

> Sandra: Yeah, he seems to see irony with the freedom message of the day.

> Nelson: I know. He keeps saying, "We are . . . we are . . ." I am sure that he is a slave.

> Amanda: I think so, too! Look at where he says, "Freedom is not his . . . isn't it astonishing that we . . ." that whole list. I bet he is a slave.

> Adrianna: Slavery is barbaric! He lists the problems in succession. "What am I to argue?" Look at the beginning of section four. It's such a big, long list of awful things.

Spirited talk occurs in all groups; anger at slavery echoes in several groups, as more agree that the speaker in the document is indeed a slave.

Ms. C glances at the clock and announces, "Unfortunately, we are out of time." A collective groan goes up, another indication of the students' engagement and investment in the reading and discussion. She assures students that they will continue the discussion tomorrow.

Careful analysis of the students' annotations after school provides Ms. C with evidence of student understanding as well as the ideas she needs to clarify. Some students are still in the noticing stage, underlining phrases and sentences that seem to indicate a point of view.

Transforming Literacy Teaching in the Era of Higher Standards © 2015 by Midge Madden and Valarie Lee, Scholastic Teaching Resources

For example, Latisha highlighted "This nation never looked blacker to me than on the fourth of July." And she noted: *The 4th of July is very colorful. So why is it dark? What does that mean? Why does he scream? And why is AMERICAN SLAVERY in all capitals? Is that a typo? Is he saying it is getting dark outside?*

Other students have moved on to interpreting the evidence presented in the speech: *Why would a writer write it this way? It must be so important for him to have a place to express his views. And where there are all capitals, I think he is yelling . . . and his words are very important . . . and a big clue that he's a slave is he sure didn't say "fellow citizens"!*

Teacher Reflection

"One-third to half of my students generally have IEPs. Some of those students go to the resource room for reading class, and others receive In-class Resource instruction. In the past, I limited reading instruction to reading class and often 'spoon fed' the required information to the class in science and social studies since I felt the students with IEPs could not read the texts. Now I look for leveled texts whenever possible and provide supports for students who struggle with textbooks. Having wonderful lessons takes so much time!

"My class took the STAR Reading assessment in September and again in January, and the class as a whole made above-average growth according to the Student Growth Percentile. The opportunities to work with texts throughout the day and in multiple subject areas has made a tremendous difference for all of my students.

"I'm trying to push kids in different ways. Before, we would have read together. Now, I'm trusting them to read themselves. There's more rigor and responsibility for students. My students with IEPs want to understand; they want to succeed. What I've discovered is that if I give them the information, with modification and differentiation, they can do it."

—Tia Cade

Side-by-Side Lesson Analysis

Framework Element	Reading Comprehension of Social Studies Textbook	Teaching Moves	Close Reading of Primary Document
Knowledge Production	Teacher provides background information and context for the speech through a video clip and slide show on abolitionists.	Provide minimal background knowledge about the speech, creating an element of discovery.	Students do not know who the speaker of the speech is. Through independent reading and partner talk, students begin to make inferences about the speaker.
Engagement	Teacher-centered discussion allows for students mostly to respond to questions the teacher poses. Video and partner talk engage the students in the beginning of lesson.	Give students 20 minutes of uninterrupted reading and talking about the speech. Facilitate by sitting in on conversations.	Students are genuinely disappointed that the discussion has to end. Students are engaged in quiet but passionate discussions and they self-monitor.
Independence	Teacher reads aloud the text to students.	Turn the task of reading over to students with adequate supports, such as audio recordings and student conferences.	Students build stamina through close reading of complex text; the majority of the reading task is turned over to students.
Voice	Turn-and-talk and teacher-led, whole-class discussion dominate the lesson. No choice provided in the lesson. There are short bursts of student conversation.	Provide space for a variety of student grouping configurations. Shift the balance so student talk outweighs teacher talk.	Partner talk and quad discussions. Students have choice in picking partners. Stamina is built through students maintaining discussions.

 Transforming Literacy Teaching in the Era of Higher Standards © 2015 by Midge Madden and Valarie Lee, Scholastic Teaching Resources

Centering Talk on Text: Are Students in Charge?

The first lesson, Inferring Character Traits From Historical Letters, is a teacher-directed lesson. The second lesson, Analyzing Character Traits Through Close Reading, focuses on student engagement and incorporates key instructional shifts such as reading, writing, and speaking grounded in evidence from both literary and informational text, building knowledge through content-rich nonfiction, and regular practice with complex text and its academic language.

Teacher-Directed Lesson:
Inferring Character Traits From Historical Letters

Students enter the classroom and quickly take their seats, arranged in groups of four. The room is crowded but inviting. Books, posters, and other resources announce the beginning of a Civil War unit. Ms. Byatt reviews homework, yesterday's discussion about abolitionists and Frederick Douglass, and refers to the courage it took to speak out against slavery. She directs students' attention to the interactive whiteboard on which she has written three questions:

- What is character?

- What is a primary source?

- How can a primary source help us better understand history?

"Hold your questions for a minute and think about William Lloyd Garrison and *The Liberator*, the speeches of Frederick Douglass, and signs posted by Harriet Tubman. Signs, speeches, letters. These are all things that were written, and they are all primary documents."

She pauses, then continues, "Today I want you to think about the three things I've listed on the interactive whiteboard. Take out a piece of paper and give it a shot. If you really don't know, you can write down, 'I'm not sure what a primary source is.' And that's OK."

Students work individually for about five minutes. Then Ms. B asks, "So, what is character?"

Raul offers, "Like what are the actions that they do?"

"Bingo!" exclaims Ms. B. "We can tell a lot about character from a person's actions. How they act, what their personality is like. So today we're going to read some primary documents to identify character traits, really to identify how people act. What's their personality like? What evidence shows the type of person they are? We will be detectives and look for evidence and clues that are written in letters."

There are a lot of puzzled expressions, and a lone hand shoots up. "I'm still kinda confused," admits Raul. Ms. B nods and smiles. "That's OK. Think, now. A primary source is what? Give me a definition. It's a little hard, I know. Anybody?"

She is met with silence. No one volunteers. Ms. B asks Sam to read what he wrote. Tentatively he reads, *A primary text is one that is harder and can get confusing but is useful in many ways.*

"Good," she nods. "But there's one more piece. Here. Listen, everyone. A primary source is an original document. An eyewitness account of an event . . . that means a person was . . ."

Sarah suggests, "There?"

"Yes!" exclaims Ms. B. "The person was there! The person lived through it. So think about this. How can a primary source help us better understand history? Who's going to be able to tell you more about slavery? Me or Frederick Douglass?"

"Frederick Douglass!" responds the class in unison.

"Absolutely!" agrees Ms. B. "Why? Talk to your neighbors."

There erupts a burst of voices as children share opinions and views. Ms. B moves about the room. She stops at Karl's table. "All right, I heard it right here. Say it again."

"He experienced it?" repeats Karl.

"He experienced it," emphasizes Ms. B. " He lived through it. So if I read Frederick Douglass' words, I can understand slavery on a much deeper level. Can letters help us understand history better?"

Class choruses, "Yes!"

Ms. B continues, "You're absolutely right." She then proceeds to tell students about her own letter file where she has saved letters for 30 or more years. She pulls out one letter written January 14, 1985, sharing that it is from her grandmother who died several years ago. She begins to read, *Grandpa and I feel good . . . we enjoyed the holidays with you all. I'm busy putting away all Christmas decorations, and everything is back in order again. . . .*

Ms. B thinks aloud, "Hmm this reminds me of my grandmom because she was always very neat." She continues, *We are bowling, and I'm giving Grandpa a hard time. I've been beating him 1–4 pins each week. I'm trying to get him to join the seniors who meet on Monday, and he hasn't made a move but is thinking about it. I'll keep trying. . . .*

Folding the letter, Ms. B asks, "So, what kind of a lady was she?" She calls on different students as they make inferences:

Anna: She seemed very nice.

Matt: She likes to bowl.

Sarah: She was determined to get Grandpa out to do things.

Ms. B nods encouragingly. "Love that word *determined*. Grandmom was the social one. Grandpa was content to be at home. Grandmom wanted to go out and get involved."

"She seemed funny with a lot of energy and everything; she tried to talk her husband into doing things," Sarah offers.

Ms. B laughs. "OK, we could say she was persistent; she didn't want to give up. Why do we know my grandmom was neat?" Several students respond, but Jared nails it when he cites, "putting Christmas decorations away."

"Good work, everyone. Now, we're starting our new unit on the Civil War and Reconstruction. And today we're going to look at traits of good character. I would have to say my grandmom was a fair, honest, and good person—she showed good character."

Ms. B distributes another letter, saying, "We're going to read a primary document written by a real person long ago. And we're going to look for character traits. I can tell you that this person also had a good, strong moral character. Our job today is to look at the letter and the evidence in the letter to try to figure out the character traits we would attribute to, or use to describe, this person. I'm not going to tell you the name of the person, not even going to tell you when the person lived, that's part of your challenge."

Students spend two to three minutes reading the first letter. Then they share in small groups what they notice. Ms. B leans in to listen to their talk.

"OK, now, all eyes here. How many think the writer is a man?" About half the class raises their hands. "Woman?" Several raise their hands. "How old?" she continues, pushing students to think.

Michael offers, "I'd say maybe thirty, 'cause, well, because the person's a good writer so older . . . mature."

"The writer had a sister," adds Sharon.

Ms. B interjects, "OK, so family is important to this person." Then she directs students to take some papers from the group basket on which 15–20 character traits are listed. Many of the words come from a reading vocabulary list. Ms. B directs students to talk in groups to define words and note words they don't know. Again, she leans in to listen to student talk.

After four to five minutes, Ms. B addresses the whole group, "OK, let's bring it together. What I'd like to do is talk about some of those challenging words and what they mean. Let's hear some."

Children volunteer *passionate*, *humble*, *ethical*, *hospitable*, *prudent*, and *tranquil*. Ms. B defines the words, one by one. She then directs, "Here's the next step. Look over the excerpt you've just read. Use a word from your vocabulary list to describe the character of the person. Write it down and note the evidence in the text. Then we are going to reread. What do good readers do?"

"Reread!" the class answers in unison.

"Right!" Ms. B then moves quickly into an explanation of what will follow after students identify character traits. She informs them that she knows a relative of the mystery letter writer. "I'm so excited about this! I'm going to put your paragraphs together into a booklet. Don't you think it will make the person feel good to see the evidence showing what good character traits this relative had?"

 Transforming Literacy Teaching in the Era of Higher Standards © 2015 by Midge Madden and Valarie Lee, Scholastic Teaching Resources

Ms. B directs students to begin. "I am seeing that some of you are finding more than one trait and that's good. You can talk and share ideas. Here's a sample prompt for your sentences: *The letter writer demonstrated he or she was compassionate because he or she worked in the hospital with wounded soldiers.* Or you can begin your paragraphs like this: *I read a letter by your relative. I believe* . . . You can quote or paraphrase, but be sure you give evidence." Ms. B tells students to focus and informs them they have about two minutes left of class.

"OK, everyone. Put the character traits sheets back in the bin. Hold on to your first sheet, your responses to the questions, and put it in your binder in a safe spot. I'll see which table is ready first. Anyone have any hints or clues as to who the mystery letter writer is?"

Students volunteer Harriet Tubman, George Washington's wife, and Frederick Douglass. They will learn in the next class that the author of the primary document was Cornelia Hancock, a nurse in the Civil War.

Teacher Reflection

"I find it [Common Core teaching] a little more freeing. . . . I can pick and choose and give myself permission to do what I know is right by kids. And we are honoring students' abilities. I'm also raising the rigor of text we read. Things that were tools before, I'm using in a different way, and kids are ready for it.

"I'm willing to take a risk . . . raising the bar a bit. I feel more empowered. I don't feel 'driven' by covering content [inch deep, mile wide principle], but rather I want to focus more on integrating literacy and social studies. We plan interdisciplinary teaching as a team. I see such value in collaborating with others, being supported by district, having a say in curriculum.

"I recognize the importance of checking in. I used to do it just to see if my students were on task. But now I have quiet conversations with my students, and I'm getting to know them in very different ways."

—Mary Byatt

✔ HOW DOES THE LESSON MEET THE STANDARDS?

Ms. B provides multiple scaffolds and strategies to help students understand the concept of primary documents:

- questions on the interactive whiteboard

- quiet thinking time before talk

- academic language

Her lesson serves as an example of a teacher beginning to experiment with including more rigorous text and more demanding expectations about what students should do with text. As a social studies teacher, she is bringing in more primary sources at a higher reading level. She clearly addresses the standards of using more informational text, increasing text complexity, and working with authentic texts. The lesson demonstrates a clear focus, albeit somewhat ambitious in terms of student expectations for one class period.

WHAT'S MISSING?

Ms. B is still experimenting with the amount of class time spent on teacher talk, which outweighs the student interaction with one another, except to respond to teacher questions. Students need more time to talk in order to process the document, including the possibility of extended group time. Ms. B has planned and delivered a well-organized lesson and provides an exemplar of a letter as a primary document (her grandmother's letter). She also provides an anonymous primary document for students to read and use to infer character traits. As students read more rigorous text, such as primary documents, they will need more time to examine the primary document in its entirety. Also, having students read multiple letters would allow them to more fully understand the character of Cornelia Hancock. The lesson has as its focus too many tasks: understanding a primary document, learning about character traits and how they give clues about a person, selecting and matching traits from a reading vocabulary list, and writing a paragraph about the yet-to-be-identified letter writer—all in 40 minutes! The standards call for teaching fewer concepts, but teaching them in more depth.

PLACING STUDENTS AT THE CORE OF A STANDARDS-BASED LESSON

As you read the next lesson, consider how Mr. Schultz:

- sets up an inquiry task as opposed to a teacher-driven task

- uses immersion in primary documents to allow students to make assumptions about the different authors

- turns more of the reading task over to students

- encourages critical thinking through close reading of text

- uses collaboration to help students move beyond individual interpretation to broader understandings about war and its human faces

Student-Centered Lesson: Analyzing Character Traits Through Close Reading

"Gather round, class," Mr. Schultz enthusiastically calls his students to the rug. "Remember our essential question for our new unit?"

Keisha waves her hand, and Mr. S smiles. "OK, Keisha, what is it?"

"Why war?" She proudly announces.

"Well done! You are correct!" Mr. S says. "And we're going to have to do some serious thinking if we really want to find the answer to our question. I'm going to start off the lesson today, but most of the time you'll be working with partners. Ready? I've put the picture book *Why?* up on our interactive whiteboard. Pay close attention as you hear the story and see the illustrations," cautions Mr. S. "There's a story here."

Students watch the illustrations from the picture book projected on the screen with rapt attention, occasionally murmuring to one another. "Hey, it's about a frog and a mouse . . . and there are no words . . . I don't get it . . . frogs and mice fighting each other?"

Mr. S listens, not saying a word. As the book ends, Mr. S challenges, "Anyone want to offer an interpretation? Just say what you're thinking."

"OK, I get the title," Jared volunteers. "*Why?* 'Why war?' is the point Popov is trying to make."

"Yep," says Mr. S. "But does the author make his point?"

"Oh, yeah, he sure does!" insists Zach. "Look at the first picture and look at the last. All war does is destroy beautiful things!"

Mr. S shows the first page again (a lovely green frog happily sitting on a giant toadstool during a brilliant blue-sky day amidst green grass and flowers) and then the last (the same frog on the same toadstool. Both the frog and toadstool are blackened and shattered, as is the surrounding countryside—colorless and destroyed).

"Why war?, indeed," he comments. "So, this book makes an important point, but we need to go deeper to understand why wars begin. Popov's book, *Why?*, is a metaphor for war—we have the mice and the frogs, but they remain nameless. We need to put a human face on wars."

Mr. S pauses, then continues, "We're beginning to study the Civil War, a terrible war where brother fought against brother. Who were these people? That's my challenge to you. We'll be reading and examining lots of primary documents to figure this out. Anyone remember what primary documents are?"

A few students nod and Sarah offers, "They're real. I mean they're kinda firsthand accounts."

Jin jumps in, "You know, they're written by people who actually lived in that time."

"Right, guys! So why are they important?"

"I think because you can depend on them," Sarah says. "They're true accounts from one person."

Mr. S adds, "So, could different documents represent different viewpoints?" The class nods yes. "You are so right, everyone. So, here's your challenge. Our essential question for the entire study is 'Why war?' I have a table filled with primary documents, and I have a cool website that you can use on

 Transforming Literacy Teaching in the Era of Higher Standards © 2015 by Midge Madden and Valarie Lee, Scholastic Teaching Resources

your tablets or laptops. Whatever you choose to read, paper or digital, they are all primary documents—written by men and women who lived during the time of the Civil War. Some are from soldiers and nurses who were in the heat of the battle. How can these documents help you get at our essential question?"

Alex suggests, "Well, we could see how different people were thinking during that time."

"Yeah," adds Zach. "If I read a letter written by a confederate soldier marching to war, maybe he'll talk about his thoughts about why he is fighting."

"Exactly!" Mr. S nods emphatically. "Now, let's get to it! Talk with your partner, choose two documents, read, then share. You can write all over these, so as you read jot down your thinking. If you're using tablets and reading digital accounts, either use the pdf comment feature or jot down notes on sticky notes."

Casey asks, "Mr. Schultz, can we make some guesses about the people? I mean like if they are Union or Confederate?"

"Absolutely," Mr. S says. "You have about thirty minutes. Then we'll all come together and see what new things we know about the people, or as I call them, the human faces of the Civil War."

Mr. S puts the website on the interactive whiteboard. Students who choose to use digital primary documents access the website through their tablets or computers. Examples of primary documents on the website include personal letters from President Lincoln, Ulysses S. Grant, Robert E. Lee, and others, in addition to personal narratives from African American soldiers.

As students read and talk quietly with partners, Mr. S moves around the room, stopping and listening in to student talk. After about 30 minutes, he signals students to reconvene on the rug for whole-group discussion.

"So, what did you find out?" he begins. "What did you learn about people who lived during the Civil War? What assumptions can you make about their characters? And how does reading personal accounts help us understand our question 'Why war?'"

"You know, Mr. Schultz," begins Zach, "I read an account by a Confederate soldier and I liked him . . . I mean I kind of even admired him. Just because he fought against the Union doesn't make him bad."

"Me, too," agrees Sarah. "I read the narratives of a Confederate nurse, and she almost convinced me that fighting for your homeland was the right thing to do."

"But, but . . ." argues Josh, "I read a letter by Lincoln, and he believed so strongly that the Union must be saved and that slavery was wrong."

Mr. S interrupts, "So, can both sides be right? Or can Confederates and Union supporters both be good people? And if so, why war? Why would good people choose to fight against one another?"

Casey raises her hand and asks, "Can a good person become so wrapped in a cause or belief that they do things like hating and killing other people?"

"Good question, Casey. Keep thinking about that." Mr. S signals that class is over, but he leaves students with a lingering question: "Think about what makes a good person. What kinds of character traits would a good person show? Tomorrow we'll revisit our primary documents, think about our assumptions about the authors, and look for evidence to back up our beliefs about whether he or she was a good person."

Side-by-Side Lesson Analysis

Framework Element	Inferring Character Traits from Historical Letters	➡ Teaching Moves	➡ Analyzing Character Traits Through Close Reading
Knowledge Production	Teacher provides primary documents. Students answer teacher-posed questions about character traits and primary documents. Teacher packs great deal of information and activities into the lesson. There is too much material to cover, and the lesson can't be finished. Teacher talk outweighs student talk.	Provide minimal background knowledge about the texts students read. Shift the focus to reading primary documents in order to make assumptions about the authors. Remain in background, inviting students to talk, share ideas, and infer whether the authors can be categorized as "good."	Students choose their own primary source texts to learn about the human face of war. They begin to understand more fully what motivates humans to choose war. Students engage in discussion to understand better the thinking of persons on both sides of the Civil War.
Engagement	Although teacher-directed, students do show interest in the letter (primary document). Turn-and-talk activities are employed to share ideas; however, the teacher provides most of the information.	Be less visible and provide more space for students to question, talk, and problem-solve. Give more opportunities to students to make choices and create their own theories about war and the people who engage in it.	Teacher uses the essential question to guide planning, then empowers students to make decisions. Students use primary documents to see perspectives on both sides of war. They make the assumptions about character as teacher observes.
Independence	Teacher directs and controls most of lesson, providing little independence.	Provide more time for students to read, talk, reflect, and come to conclusions about the letter writer.	Students select texts (primary documents) and make their own assumptions and inferences about the authors. Teacher acts as facilitator, when necessary.
Voice	Teacher-led, whole-class discussion dominates the lesson, with only short bursts of student conversation.	Provide more time for students to interact with one another and more opportunities for students to articulate their learning.	Students direct the learning. Make themselves heard through choice, sharing of ideas, and collaborative analyses of primary documents.

Transforming Literacy Teaching in the Era of Higher Standards © 2015 by Midge Madden and Valarie Lee, Scholastic Teaching Resources

Chapter 2

Inviting Students to Talk About Literature

"Reading and writing float on a sea of talk."
—James Britton (1970)

Much talk about teaching changes suggested by the Common Core State Standards focuses on reading. Topics such as complex texts, close readings, informational texts, and identifying textual evidence seem to occupy much of the national conversation. Speaking and listening, although one of the four basic strands, have received much less attention. But should they? We believe that speaking and listening are the foundation upon which reading and writing are built; improving the ability to use oral language helps students to read and write better.

If literacy levels are to improve, the aims of the English Language Arts classroom, especially in the earliest grades, must include oral language in a purposeful, systematic way, in part because it helps students master the printed word. Besides having intrinsic value as modes of communication, listening and speaking are necessary prerequisites of reading and writing.

(Common Core State Standards, 2010, Appendix A. p. 27)

Further perusal of the speaking and listening strand shows an emphasis on collaborative conversations. Speaking and listening standards call for students to engage effectively in a range of collaborative discussions. They state that although formal presentations are one way that talk occurs, students must also have opportunities to engage in informal conversations as they collaborate to answer questions and build understanding of new content knowledge. This becomes particularly critical in the middle school grades where students need to learn to speak the languages of the various disciplines (science, social studies, math, literature, etc.). Student learning must not be limited to simply reading texts and writing in response; rather, it can be deepened and further advanced through conversation. Discussion about important ideas can lead to better understanding, reframing, and clarification. When students speak and listen carefully to one another, they often learn through an immediacy of expression and many voices can be heard.

All of the lessons in this chapter have some form of speaking and listening as their main focus. The first set of lessons uses literature circles to discuss the novel *The Devil's Arithmetic* by Jane Yolen. The second set of lessons looks at student talk and the importance of textual support in studying the novel *Tangerine* by Edward Bloor.

Deepening Literature Conversations:
Is the Conversation Authentic?

The first lesson, Literature Circle Roles, is a teacher-directed lesson. The second lesson, Collaborative Literature Discussions, incorporates key instructional shifts such as regular practice with complex text and reading and speaking from evidence. Furthermore, students voice their deep understandings of text through collaborative discussion.

Teacher-Directed Lesson:
Literature Circle Roles

"Time for lit circles," Ms. Berrigan announces. *The Devil's Arithmetic* group, I'll meet with you first. Remember to bring your book packets and role assignment papers." Six students pull up chairs at the kidney-shaped table, balancing books, laminated role-direction cards, response journals, scheduling forms for meeting dates, and reading and role assignments. "Whew! This is a lot of stuff to remember," murmurs Jared. "What I really want to do is just talk about our book, you know? I'm already into it . . . on chapter five!"

Sarah exclaims, "Jared, you're not supposed to read ahead! We're discussing chapters one and two."

Jared sighs, "Oh, I know, I know, but when a book is good, I just have to keep reading!"

"Hmmm, so you like the book, Jared?" Ms. B settles into her chair. "That's good." She smiles and asks the group, "Everyone know their roles? Remember to use our chart if you need to." She directs students' attention to the posted chart:

Student Roles

❖ Discussion Director

❖ Literary Luminary

❖ Illustrator/Mapper

❖ Word Wizard

❖ Connector

❖ Investigator

"Rosemarie, you're the Discussion Director. We'll start with you."

Rosemarie begins, "Well, I used the questions you gave us in our packet, Ms. Berrigan. But maybe next time I can think of my own."

"OK, that's fine." Ms. B smiles. "Go on, Rosemarie. Share them with us, and we'll see if we can answer them." Rosemarie reads the questions:

- What is on Grandpa Will's arm? Why do you think it's there?

- Why, according to Grandma Belle, does the family continue to play the traditional holiday games?

- Who do you think is in the field at the end of the chapter? Why do you think that?

Then she picks different students to respond. Ms. B. guides students as they respond, helping them find evidence in their books to support their answers.

"Good work, group! Let's go on to our next role. Who is Literary Luminary?" Ms. B asks. "That's me," says Braden. "I found a really cool quote. Can I read it?" "Absolutely," says Ms. B. Braden turns to his copy, finds his sticky note where he recorded the quote, and begins:

When she'd been younger, the five-digit number on his arm had fascinated her. It was a dark blue very much like a stain. The skin around it had gotten old, but the number had not. (p. 9)

"Excellent choice," praises Ms. B. "Now, next . . . who is the Illustrator?"

"Oh, that's me," volunteers Betty Jo. "I made a drawing."

Ryan waves his hand. "I know, I know! It's a yarmulke! The little hats that Jewish men and boys wear—but I don't know why they do." Eric adds, "Well, everyone, I mean all the males, wears them in the first chapter. Even Grandpa Will."

Ms. B. interrupts, "Good noticing, boys, but can anyone tell me the importance of yarmulkes? Anyone?" Ryan shakes his head. "I don't know why, Ms. Berrigan. I just thought it was a tradition that was passed down from father to son."

"That's a good guess or hunch, Ryan. This is something we should all look up for our next meeting."

Ms. B then asks the Word Wizard and Connector to explain their findings. When they finish sharing, she calls on Joanna. "You were the Investigator for these first three chapters. Tell us what you found out about the Holocaust and the author of *The Devil's Arithmetic*."

Joanna hesitates, then in a faltering voice begins, "Well, I asked my dad about the Holocaust and what it was. He said he couldn't explain it to me—I was too young. Then he asked me why I wanted to know and what I was reading. I started to tell him about our new book but he just left the room, muttering about the things kids today read in schools. I don't get it, Ms. Berrigan. I mean, this is a good book, isn't it? And Jane Yolen is a famous author, right?"

Ms. B nods. "Joanne, you're absolutely right, but sometimes people don't understand why it's important to learn about the past, even if terrible things happened. As we continue reading and talking about our book, things will become clearer to you. We'll be studying World War II in social studies, so learning about Hitler and Germany will give you more background information to help you understand what the Holocaust and . . . oh my goodness, look at the time! Such a good discussion, but now we're way over lit circle time. Be sure to get your role assignments for the next two chapters, and we'll talk more at our next meeting."

✔ HOW DOES THE LESSON MEET THE STANDARDS?

When reflecting upon Ms. B's implementation of literature circles in her classroom, we can see that students clearly understand the various roles of each group member. Ms. B has built in multiple supports to ensure an organized book discussion. Students are given laminated role description cards, response journals, and discussion rules handouts. There is also some collaborative effort to understand the text more fully during the discussion.

Transforming Literacy Teaching in the Era of Higher Standards © 2015 by Midge Madden and Valarie Lee, Scholastic Teaching Resources

Students come to the literature circle with clipboards in hand and assigned role responsibilities completed. The group runs smoothly; one by one students inform the others what they have discovered in their reading. In sharing their assigned role findings, students do talk about their book and listen to one another. Thus, they appear to be engaged—trying to understand the plot and important characters. In keeping with the standards, students seem to have some ownership. They prepare for discussion, albeit constrained by the required role assignments. Yet the group discussion is more than a series of teacher-posed questions where students must guess the answer the teacher has in her mind. The role assignments may be the teacher's, but the work remains the students'—until they are proven wrong. Yet, teaching the Holocaust, in this case to fifth graders, might seem a daunting task to many teachers. As such, Ms. B deserves credit for attempting to introduce such a sensitive subject.

WHAT'S MISSING?

Because Ms. B controls the conversation by calling on students to contribute according to their role assignments, there is little natural conversation around the text. It seems as if Ms. B stoically pushes on; in the interest of time, she decides that completing the lesson is more important than ensuring full understanding of the story events. There is clearly a need for more background information. The discussion suggests that there is some basic misunderstanding about the story and the characters. Collaborative group meaning also seems to be missing in this lesson. Ms. B remains in control throughout the lesson. There is little spontaneous discussion or thinking while speaking; students know and follow the rules they have been given.

PLACING STUDENTS AT THE CORE OF A STANDARDS-BASED LESSON

As you read the next lesson, consider how Ms. Carhart:

- encourages students to dig deeper and share their ideas

- creates a space for students to listen to one another

- uses provocative or critical texts, which leads students to engage and generate profound questions about the characters and human nature

Student-Centered Lesson:
Collaborative Literature Discussions

Strains of classical music play softly in the background against the hushed murmur of fifth graders. Talk begins in a corner of the room where seven students sit cross-legged on pillows, *The Devil's Arithmetic* and clipboards on their laps. Holden is explaining how book club scheduling goes.

"It's really cool, guys," Holden begins. "See that big chart over there? We make our own reading assignments and schedule our book club meetings. We have to agree on how much to read, what to write about in our response journals, and promise to come to meetings really prepared!"

Ms. Carhart gently interrupts, "Thanks, Holden. We can talk more about that after our meeting today. Now, who's ready to begin?"

Ellis waves his hand, and Ms. C nods.

"It's just plain stupid," he angrily protests. "It doesn't make any sense."

Ms. C holds up her hand. "*Stupid*'s a harsh word, Ellis. Why would you choose that?"

"Well," Ellis argues, "you're . . . you're just reliving the whole Holocaust. Who would want to do that? Why would you watch a video to see it all again?"

"Hmmm," Ms. C replies. "What reaction did he have, Ellis?"

"He was yelling at the TV, and umm . . . I don't know, he was just mad."

"Well, why was he yelling? If his action was stupid, why? Go back and look in the chapter. We'll come back to you." Ms. C says reassuringly.

"Umm, well I wouldn't call him stupid." Sarah holds out two fingers (the signal to add further comments). Pushing her glasses back, she continues, "I'd just say he wasn't thinking at that time. Because what they said . . . why we wanted to rewatch—it was just a bad time. Why would they relive and watch the whole video? I don't think anybody would want to remember that day, and if you escaped you were lucky to."

Jerry interrupts, "Was it just a day, Sarah?"

"Well, it was a long time, more than a day."

   Transforming Literacy Teaching in the Era of Higher Standards © 2015 by Midge Madden and Valarie Lee, Scholastic Teaching Resources

Five students all wave two fingers. Ms. C points to Jayden.

"Well, kind of what we were saying. It says on page 9, well, on page 8: 'Then she murmured, "Please forgive him, please. It was the war." Her voice was as soft as a prayer.'"

Several others signal that they have something to say. Ms. C nods to Casey. "I get it, I think. The grandfather is a survivor of the Holocaust, and when he remembers, all of the anger he holds inside just comes out. It's kind of a confusing way to begin a book, though. Why would the author do that?"

"Excellent thinking!" exclaims Ms. C. "Why indeed? You guys are now not only thinking about the story and the plot, but you're questioning the writing moves, or decisions, of the author. We've only read the first chapter and it is really, really confusing. Take a few moments now, go over your notes, and let's try to figure this out. Ask yourselves if this first chapter is a good way to begin the story, and why or why not."

As Ms. C watches the group, she takes notes on her clipboard. Two girls whisper, sharing their comments. Ellis frowns as he rereads the final words of the chapter. Then his face brightens as understanding dawns. "I get it, now I get it," he bursts out. The group laughs, and Ms. C smiles. "OK, Ellis. Go ahead."

Ellis grins and explains, "Well, actually, it is a very cool way to begin a book! It's like, you know, the book where the kids go through a door into another world."

"Oh, you mean like *The Lion, the Witch and the Wardrobe*?" Casey interrupts. "Yeah, yeah, just like that. I think the author—Jane Yolen, right?—anyway, I think she wants to start us in the present with someone who doesn't get the Holocaust at all, and then take her back in time."

"I think you're right," Casey agrees. "And I think the author is pretty smart because I want to keep reading to find out where, or what, this new world is."

"Me, too," add a few others. "This is going to be a pretty awesome book!"

Casey looks at the clock and announces, "Uh oh, our time's up. How much do we want to read before our next meeting?"

"The whole book!" laughs Ellis.

"Seriously," Casey responds. "And we have to write journal and blog responses, too, so don't forget."

Sarah suggests, "Well, Ms. Carhart said we have to be finished reading the book in three weeks. So let's split up the book that way. We meet every three days so we can read two chapters, note our thinking, write, and be ready to talk." The group agrees, replaces the pillows in the reading corner, and returns to their tables.

"Nice work, today, everyone," Ms. C comments. "I'll be curious to read and hear your thinking as we get deeper into the book. And you've got a good plan of action. Keep asking those tough questions and bring them to group next time."

Teacher Reflection

"You can't worry about time if you want kids to get deep meaning of texts. They have to talk and puzzle ideas out individually and together. That's the power of my lit circles, I think. I let students run with an idea, chase down the evidence in their texts, and talk and talk until they get it. It's all Common Core stuff that I've always done. I just believe when you use books that have big ideas about things that matter to kids, they will want to learn!"

— Kathy Carhart

Side-by-Side Lesson Analysis

Framework Element	Literature Circle Roles	Teaching Moves	Collaborative Literature Discussions
Knowledge Production	Teacher assigns roles and has students complete role sheets. Teacher-directed discussion controls meaning-making. Students share by their role assignments, and have little natural conversation around the text.	Facilitate, rather than direct, discussion. Solicit and value students' thinking. Place a clear importance on using textual evidence to support interpretation.	Students create knowledge about text through their own questions and discussions. Students use evidence from text to support their responses.
Engagement	Students complete role worksheets and answer teacher-posed questions.	Allow more time to talk about emerging meaning in text. Encourage more student-generated questions and back-and-forth talk among students.	All students contribute to the discussion, using finger codes to indicate whether expanding ideas or offering new ideas on new topic. Student-generated questions may not be easily answered (e.g., *Why do we have war? Why would the Germans let so many Jews be killed?*), but an attempt should be made.
Independence	Teacher directs both the work and the discussion.	Move from assigned roles to encouraging conversation about the text. Let students talk; deeper meaning emerges through conversation. Interrupt to clarify only if absolutely necessary.	Teacher role is that of facilitator, clarifying when necessary. Discussion is initiated and controlled by the students in the book club. Students take responsibility for setting the schedule for group meetings, assigning the chapters to be read, and journaling responses.
Voice	Teacher directs student talk, and there is more teacher talk than student talk.	Hand over more responsibility for discussion to students.	Discussion clearly highlights students' voices. Teacher voice is in background, offering support as needed.

Listening in on Discussions: Can Students Learn From My Feedback?

The first lesson, Evidence-Based Discussion, is a teacher-directed lesson. The second lesson, Marker-Talk Discussion, incorporates key instructional shifts such as regular practice with complex text and reading, writing, and speaking from evidence. Furthermore, choice plays a critical role in engagement with literature.

Teacher-Directed Lesson: Evidence-Based Discussion

"OK, everybody, you should be in your groups now, looking at the questions. Begin to talk about possible responses to each question."

Mr. Rivera's classroom is alive with conversations as students are moving, talking to one another, arguing about questions, and looking for textual evidence to prove their points. Four large poster sheets with 10 to 15 higher-level questions are each posted around the room, and students huddle in groups around each poster. Examples include:

- What does it mean for Paul to be a Tangerine Middle School War Eagle?

- Why do you think Paul is so successful at Tangerine Middle School, while Joey can't handle the new atmosphere?

- What did Luis Cruz mean to Paul? Explain.

The novel *Tangerine* by Edward Bloor can be seen on student desks. The classroom hums with student talk, and most students participate in the activity.

Melinda, who has arrived late to class, asks her group members, "What are we supposed to be doing?"

Takia offers, "Well, he put us in these groups and gave us these questions."

Zach jumps in. "We had to answer the questions for homework. Now we're supposed to work in our groups to compare our answers. Then we'll move around and read everyone else's responses to see if we agree."

"Oh. . . ." Melinda says. "Do we need our books?"

"Nah," Zach replies. "We just have to write what we think."

"All right, guys, let's quiet down," requests Mr. R. "Sounds like you are having some lively discussions, but let's be sure we're all getting the work done." He addresses each group, asking them how many questions they have covered. A handful of students have their novel packets with the homework questions answered.

Susan whispers to Manny, "Are we supposed to have all these questions answered?" He nods, and smiles sheepishly. "Well, yeah. But there's always someone in the group who's done the homework."

Suddenly the lights dim, and Mr. R says, "OK, groups, time's up. Let's see what we've got."

He moves from group to group, reading aloud responses from the poster sheets and asking questions, inviting discussion. Four or five students dominate the talk while the rest of the class simply listens. Some have their homework packets open, a few thumb through the novel, but most sit idly, watching the clock.

"Bell's about to ring," Takia murmurs, packing up her books.

Mr. R stops talking and looks at the clock. He announces, "For homework tomorrow, read the next three chapters in *Tangerine* and answer the questions in your packet. We'll continue discussion next class."

✔ HOW DOES THE LESSON MEET THE STANDARDS?

Mr. R attempts to establish a conversation about *Tangerine* and uses higher-level questions from his teaching materials to push his students to go deeper in analyzing plot and characters. By getting students out of their seats and writing on the charts, he strives to engage all his students in interacting with the text and with their peers.

🔍 WHAT'S MISSING?

Although students are up and moving around during their conversations, the questions they answer are teacher-generated and do not necessarily reflect the questions students have about the text. Also, while several students are engaged in the discussion, many are merely listening in.

PLACING STUDENTS AT THE CORE OF A STANDARDS-BASED LESSON

As you read the next lesson, consider how Mr. Nakia:

- centers the conversation around students' questions derived from their book clubs

- engages students to use evidence from the text to support key points

- uses the marker-talk discussion strategy to engage all students

- monitors and facilitates the discussion, helping students who struggle get to deeper comprehension

Student-Centered Lesson: Marker-Talk Discussion

The bell rings for third hour as the students take their seats. Students come to the class with their *Tangerine* texts marked with sticky notes and highlights.

Mr. Nakia says, "OK everyone. You know we've been working on chapters three and four. And remember, we've been using the big, guiding questions we developed to help us stay focused on the text."

He points to an anchor chart listing the questions:

- How does Bloor create tension and interest through his use of foreshadowing?

- What is complex about the relationship between Paul and his dad?

- How can we use prediction to further our understanding of the book?

Mr. N continues, "Remember, yesterday I asked you to go onto our class document share site and list at least two questions you would like to discuss related to chapters three and four. Last night, I went through the doc and finalized the list. Your questions are amazing! I had to delete some of the questions because they were more fact-based, yes-or-no type questions, but most of them were the big, ponderable type of questions we have been discussing."

"Our next step is that each book club is going to select one of the questions you generated." He projects the document on the screen. "Each book club has a piece of chart paper on the wall behind them. Quickly decide as a group on a question, and let me know. Then write the question on your chart paper."

Vince shouts out, "Our group wants this question: *Why do you think the dad overlooks many things about the family and the move?*" Mr. N deletes it from the list. After all the groups have chosen their question, he gives the next directions.

"You spent some time reading and thinking with your pen yesterday, marking the text for possible evidence. For this next part, I am going to warn you: This isn't going to be like discussions you are used to! What makes it different is that I don't want you to talk in the beginning!"

The students look at each other with puzzled expressions.

"I know, that seems weird, but there's a reason. I want everyone in the group to have an opportunity to write their thoughts before everyone starts talking. It gives me a chance to see what you bring to the discussion and gives every member a chance to contribute. Can we try this out? Here's a colored marker for each of you. You will respond to your group's question by writing a response, writing a quote from the book as evidence, or writing any other thing you are thinking." Mr. N models this with the document projector. "So, if someone wrote, 'I think the dad is acting this way because of his own insecurities,' I could agree and write a statement, disagree and say why, or add a quote from the text to support it. The expectation is that everyone will write something and keep writing until I say stop."

He gives them the OK to start and the silent discussion begins. In Group 1, Vince begins by writing on the group's chart paper: *The dad really overlooked the problems with the neighborhood because he was more concerned about his son playing football.* Simultaneously, Selena is writing down a quote from the book. Richie says, "What about putting something about . . ." but Selena quickly stops him, "Hey, we're not supposed to talk yet!"

Mr. N walks over and redirects Richie, writing on the chart, *What do you think?* Richie starts writing, *I think the dad is misunderstood because . . .*, and Mr. N continues to walk around, monitoring group members as they write. He notices that Manuel is slouched down in his chair, without his book open. Mr. N redirects him back to the book and notices he has minimal markings. He takes Manuel back to the page with the quote, whispering, "Manuel, I want you to read this again and see if you can add something to your group's question. What do you think the dad has overlooked? Look for some evidence, and when I come back in a few minutes, I will check to see how you did." After noting this on his class chart, he moves to the next group.

After five minutes, he calls for the groups to stop and look up front. "OK folks! Here's your challenge now. You are going to shift over to the right to the next chart. As a group, you have to look over the question, read what the other group wrote, and challenge yourself to expand upon their ideas. For instance, What is another example from the book you could offer to support something they said? What is another way of looking at the question that they didn't consider? Where do you disagree with them? Again, try and provide some support for any new ideas you add to the chart. What other text-based evidence from *Tangerine* can you add to the chart?"

Selena jumps right in, writing, *You said that the dad has overlooked how competitive the sports would be in Florida, but I think he knew that all along! He's so weird about his son being the best at football.* Richie reads what she is writing and responds below her writing, *I guess, but I still think he had no idea it would be THAT competitive.* Mr. N is observing and writes on the chart, *What could you find in the text that would support either or both perspectives?* He moves on as Selena and Richie go back to the text.

Mr. N moves back to Manuel's original group chart and notices that he had added a response to the question, but Mr. N recognizes that Manuel is still struggling. Mr. N follows him to the next chart and observes how he interacts with it, noticing how hesitant he is and how difficult it is for him to come up with a way to respond to what others are writing. Mr. N wonders if it is lack of comprehension, engagement, or preparation. He makes a note to himself to investigate this further.

Transforming Literacy Teaching in the Era of Higher Standards © 2015 by Midge Madden and Valarie Lee, Scholastic Teaching Resources

Each group moves from chart to chart, reading others' comments and adding their own, finally ending up at their original chart. Mr. N comments, "Wow, even though it was quiet in here, I was amazed at how I could almost hear you thinking, agreeing, and reflecting as you wrote! I noticed that everyone made an attempt to write some response to the questions. Some of you had more evidence, but I noticed almost all of you went back into the text at some point."

Then he asks each group to read and consider all the responses, evidence, and comments from their original chart. Each group discusses the responses and works to write a collaborative synthesis of the responses. They share this statement with the rest of the class. Finally, he asks the students to debrief on the lesson.

Richie volunteers, "It was hard not to talk, but I finally got it."

"Yeah," Melinda agrees. "But I liked that we couldn't talk. Sometimes you can't even say a word without someone jumping in!"

Mr. N smiles and nods, "What I liked best about it was that I watched each one of you think about the questions and write a response. Sometimes, it's easy to get lost in the discussion and not really have a chance to respond. Every one of you had something to say about *Tangerine*, and almost all of you used evidence from the text to support your ideas.

"Well, done, everybody!

"Now, as you read the next two chapters, think about this evidence piece and how you can support your thinking in our next class discussions."

Side-by-Side Lesson Analysis

Framework Element	Evidence-Based Discussion	➡ Teaching Moves ➡	Marker-Talk Discussion
Knowledge Production	Teacher provides questions about the novel from a commercial study guide.	Create a shared class document for students to use to submit questions in advance of the lesson.	Students create questions based on their reading.
Engagement	Teacher actively engages a few students in discussing the novel.	Use marker-talk and student movement around charts to increase the interaction of all students.	All students contribute both in silent talk and group synthesis.
Independence	Students write from what they know, what they remember. Some students use the text for evidence, but many do not.	Emphasize the importance of rereading and of having all students participate in the discussion. Monitor and assess students' progress to help students move to greater independence.	Students must use knowledge and evidence from the text to contribute. Expectation is that all students will contribute.
Voice	Students leave the classroom without giving feedback on their understanding.	Have students select a question from their list and ensure all students have an equal opportunity to contribute responses.	Student voices are heard in a whole-class debriefing and in quick one-on-one teacher conferences (with struggling students).

Chapter 3

Writing With Purpose

> "The Common Core State Standards have set the bar to a height that no one teacher, no single year of teaching, can attain. Young writers grow as oak trees do, over years . . ."
>
> —Lucy Calkins (2010)

Today's standards place a greater emphasis on writing to argue and explain; narrative writing remains important, but less so than in the past. We might think of this shift in terms of a new organization of writing applications into three major categories:

- opinion (K–5) or argument (6–12)

- informative/explanatory

- narrative

Yet teachers must use caution when interpreting this shift from narrative to more argumentative/informational writing. What is important is that students see the purpose for writing in many genres. The International Reading Association

(IRA) and the National Council of Teachers of English (NCTE) argue that teachers must not forget what we have learned over the years about good writing practices. Effective writing instruction has stressed the importance of process and developing pieces over time, a focus on student choice, and writing for real and meaningful purposes. Students must learn to recognize and consider the many and varied purposes for writing and fit their writing to each purpose.

In keeping with the goal of authentic writing for real audiences, teachers need to find ways to move student writing beyond classroom walls. Technology and today's global and digital world offer many possibilities to broadcast student writing into the world. Equally important, the CCSS call for writing in many different domains as well as in and across disciplines. Students need to use multiple genres of writing, and writing tasks need to be increasingly attached to texts. For example, students might include imaginative and nonfiction genres in a narrative piece of writing about a period in history. CCSS writing shifts become more inclusive of reading, speaking, and listening. Writing must be attached to textual evidence, and it must also be spoken and listened to by wider audiences. Collaborative writing becomes regular practice as students become engaged in inquiry projects around complex questions.

The four lessons in this chapter focus on writing and show in some way the integration of reading, writing, speaking, and listening.

Providing Guidance:
How Much Support Do Students Need?

The first lesson, Introduction to the Causes of World War I, is a teacher-directed lesson. The second lesson, Dramatizing History, incorporates key instructional shifts such as regular practice with complex text and building knowledge through content-rich nonfiction.

Teacher-Directed Lesson:
Introduction to the Causes of World War I

"Please take out your textbooks," Mr. Barker directs the students in his second period social studies class. "We're launching our study of World War I today. So, grab a laptop or a tablet and get into your study groups." As students ready for the lesson, Mr. B posts the lesson objectives on the interactive whiteboard:

Understand the diverse long-range causes of World War I including:

- political and economic rivalries

- ethnic and ideological conflicts

- militarism, imperialism, and nationalism

- how nationalism threatened the balance of power among the Great Powers in Europe, and why it was considered one of the causes of World War I

Mr. B then directs students to share what they know about World War I. He records student responses on a slide in a PowerPoint presentation. Some students have seen the movie *War Horse*; others have watched the History Channel or read biographies of leaders during that time period (e.g., President Wilson, Archduke Ferdinand, Chancellor Bismarck, General Patton). The students' responses include trench warfare, Archduke Ferdinand's assassination, and the sinking of the *Lusitania*.

"Not bad for a beginning," comments Mr. B. "Today we're going to explore further to see what we can learn about some of the events that led up to World War I—we can think of these events as causes for the war." He pulls up a list of links to relevant websites.

"Here's what I want you to do. Work in groups, go to one or two of these websites, and look through them. You'll find print information, video clips, and photos. See what you can find about more causes. As you search the Internet, you may find other sites as well. Feel free to use any site but be sure to track where you get your information on an inquiry chart."

Inquiry Chart—downloadable pdf is available online (see page 16)

Kara raises her hand and asks, "Can we each search on our tablets? Then put together our ideas?"

"Yep, that's fine," responds Mr. B. "I'll come around, too, to see how you're doing."

Familiar with how to use tablets and the Internet, students get right to work. "Hey, check out this clip," exclaims Ali. "It's really cool! Shows soldiers in trenches, gas masks. . . ." Working individually at first, students gradually move into groups as they share findings.

"Mr. Barker," Gina announces, "I didn't know much at all about this war. Our textbook last year made it so boring. I just memorized some facts and then forgot them. But this is awesome!"

"Yeah," agrees Reed. "I mean I'm kinda surprised that they even have video of these times. How'd they get it? Did they even have movie cameras then?"

"That's a good question, Reed," Mr. B admits. "Something to figure out. And that makes me think of something else. As you check out websites, see who wrote them. Is the information accurate? What about the video clips? Are they real or re-enacted? All things you should be considering when you use a website. Is it accurate, and how do you know?"

Students continue working, intermittently calling out things they've found. Mr. B reminds, "Be sure you're tracking your research. Remember you'll have to show others the evidence for each cause you list." After 40 minutes, Mr. B announces, "Okay everyone, time's up. Let's see what you have."

As students volunteer information they found, Mr. B lists it on the interactive whiteboard. When he finishes, he challenges, "OK, talk in your groups to see which you think are primary causes of the war. Ten minutes!" Talk fills the classroom. Students argue about which events to include, trying to agree within their groups. "Got a consensus?" Mr. B asks. "Let's share out."

Groups volunteer the assassination of Archduke Ferdinand, imperialism, and territory fights.

Mr. B comments, "You have listed some causes, but there are others. I'm going to add some that you missed. Then you'll need to decide as a group which cause you want to investigate further."

"What if we don't know about a cause?" Jared asks.

"You'll just have to research it," responds Mr. B.

Jake questions, "I found imperialism but I have no clue what that it means!" Others nod in agreement.

Mr. B responds, "This is an inquiry. I want you to find the answers."

"But, but, how can we, if we don't understand the research?" Jake persists. "Some of these websites must be written for people who are experts in history."

"Figure it out, Jake. Just do your best," replies Mr. B.

"Decided on a cause?" Mr. B asks. Group members nod yes, and he continues. "Good! Now I want you to go back to different sites to collect detailed information about your particular cause. Take lots of notes and begin to draft a narrative of your cause, really a summary of the cause or event that led to World War I. You can use photos, too, to add to your narrative. Tomorrow you'll finish your writing. Then you'll post all of your narratives and photos. We can post our writing outside in our hall or create a digital timeline. You will decide."

Several hands go up. "No questions," Mr. B. states. "Just start to work and see what you find."

Students go off, talking in groups. Several voices are heard, talking quietly. "I have no idea what we're doing," murmurs Reed.

✔ HOW DOES THE LESSON MEET THE STANDARDS?

Although the final assignment is teacher-directed, Mr. B engages students and pushes them to explore causes for World War I. He invites students to conduct Internet research to build knowledge. Here, he moves beyond the traditional social studies textbook lesson where students read and answer end-of-chapter questions. Mr. B also lectures minimally, providing class time for students to read, think, and talk out ideas. He does require students to complete a worksheet, and students have a required summary essay for the final writing product. This lesson addresses many of the standards, such as infusing technology, reading multiple texts critically, and informational writing.

WHAT'S MISSING?

The lesson is ambitious in that it assumes that all students will be able to extract important ideas across multiple websites and combine them to understand the causes of World War I. It requires students to be able to analyze and synthesize texts, photos, and videos, but lacks the supports for those students who may struggle. In this case, the teacher may be providing too little direction. Based upon students' confusion, it seems as if more teacher direction would be helpful. In trying to give students more independence, Mr. B fails to provide student support when needed. How is Mr. B assessing individual understanding? Students clearly learn something about World War I from exploring websites, which are good sources of information. But one of the challenges of teaching is meeting the needs of all students, and it is not clear how, or whether, Mr. B accomplishes this.

PLACING STUDENTS AT THE CORE OF A STANDARDS-BASED LESSON

As you read the next lesson, consider how Mr. Cooper:

- integrates reading, writing, and speaking
- builds in supports to meet needs of all students
- uses kinds of informal assessment
- provides choices, which contribute to student success

Transforming Literacy Teaching in the Era of Higher Standards © 2015 by Midge Madden and Valarie Lee, Scholastic Teaching Resources

Student-Centered Lesson:
Dramatizing History

"OK, class, welcome to 1914!" Mr. Cooper's eyes sweep the room, making sure all his students are listening. "We're going back in time today, trying to visualize what it would have been like to live during that time. But first, who can tell me what we did yesterday?"

Hands fly up. Mr. C nods at Jerome. "Well, we, uh, we talked about the war. You know, what caused it, who made it happen, that sort of stuff."

"OK, good. Anyone else?" Mr. C asks.

Sally adds, "We did a K-W-L chart to see what we already knew. Oh, and we got vocabulary words to learn."

"Right!" says Mr. C. "And I showed you all a PowerPoint on the causes of World War I, remember? You took notes, and then we talked and added to our class K-W-L." Mr. C pauses. "Let's review what we learned yesterday." He pulls up the K-W-L chart on the interactive whiteboard and quickly reads. He then continues, "So, think about what you know so far. Talk to one another for a few minutes. If you had to be a person fighting in World War I or living in England during that time, what would you have to know?"

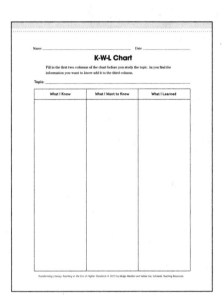

K-W-L Chart—downloadable pdf is available online (see page 16)

In pairs and groups of three, students talk animatedly about Mr. C's question. "Guess we'd have to know more than just causes of the war," comments Sally. "Yeah," Felicia adds. "But, I mean, how can we be someone if we don't know about him?"

Mr. C interrupts Felicia, "Good thinking, Felicia! Anybody have ideas about this? If you had to become a person from long ago and didn't know a thing about him or her, what could you do?"

Mr. C smiles, recognizing a student who definitely "gets" it. "Inner monologue. That's right, Luke. And I think you're on to a plan. You know you have to understand the inner and outer person, right? Everybody got that? Any questions so far?" He leans back against his desk. "No? OK, then, hold that thought for a minute. Now, change your focus from a person to an event. What would you have to do to act out an event? Talk it out."

"Man, I don't know about an event. How *are* we going to decide that?" Nat shakes his head. "Shoot," Kerry says. "Same way. You read about it and maybe even read about the people who were in the event. I guess you could find a video, too, and some photos. Lots of good websites to search."

Students in various groups agree that they'd have to do research and make some assumptions based on the facts. Mr. C then asks how they would act out their event. And how they would get from a collection of facts to a dramatic performance of a real historical event.

"Man, that's kinda hard," murmurs Ryan. "I don't know anything about acting out."

"Are you kidding?" quips Luke. "All you ever do is act out!" The class bursts into laughter.

"OK, everyone, get serious." Mr. C smiles. "I want you to think hard. Actually, I'm going to show a clip from a movie to help you get started. Has anybody seen *War Horse* or read the book?"

Several students raise hands. "Awesome movie!" exclaims Ryan.

"Can anyone give us a synopsis?" ask Mr. C.

Ryan responds, "Well, it's about a horse. Kind of a story of a horse who actually fights in World War I. But I think it's also about what it was like in those times. Gives you a good idea of what soldiers went through."

"Good!" Mr. C nods. "So watch this clip, and we'll talk afterward. It's one event in the movie." He plays the scene where the horse, Joey, wanders into "no man's land." Joey is seriously wounded and near death with little strength left. He is trapped in barbed wire and thrashing to free himself. A Welshman and a German wave white flags and meet to toss a coin to see who will rescue Joey.

Students watch with rapt attention. They clap at the end of the clip. "That was amazing." Sarah shakes her head. "Did that really happen?"

"Well," explains Mr. C, "that's what we call fictionalizing an event in history—making it into a story and dramatizing it. They did use horses in World War I, though I'm not sure everything in the movie is true. But that's what you're going to do—you'll take an event and figure out how to act it out. Of course, we don't have Hollywood to help us [students laugh], but you can use props, music, whatever to help us see your event."

"Awesome," exclaims Nat. "How much time we got, Mr. C?"

Mr. C counters, "How much time do you think you'll need? Talk. Then we'll get a consensus. But let me give you the game plan. You're going to work in your groups to puzzle this out. You can pick any event in history—world history, ancient history, American history. You're going to research that event and become an expert. Then you'll work together to write a script for your performance from all the notes you've written. I need to approve your draft; then you'll type the revised script, practice it, and perform."

Mr. C then goes to the interactive whiteboard and pulls up a worksheet to help in the planning to dramatize history.

"A couple of more things," he explains. "Your dramatizations can be done in many different styles, including a staged reading, a play, or a podcast. Once you write your scripts, I'll give you a day or two to work on your performances. You need to be as accurate to the time period as possible. How should the dialogue sound? Will you dress in costumes that mimic the time period? Will you use any background music appropriate to the time?"

Students confer and decide they need the week to research, write the scripts, and practice. Performances are scheduled for the following Monday.

Dramatizing History Planning Sheet— downloadable pdf is available online (see page 16)

"OK, class, let's begin," Mr. C says. "You have the rest of the period to brainstorm your event and begin researching. I want to know at the end of class what person or event each group has selected. Oh, and by the way, I asked Mrs. Soloman's class and Mr. Madden to come see your final performances!"

"No way!" exclaims Ryan. "Cool!"

At the close of the period, Mr. C calls each group and lists their event or character on a classroom chart. Final selections are recorded:

Group 1: Michelangelo painting the Sistine Chapel

Group 2: The Last Supper

Group 3: George Washington at Valley Forge

Group 4: Abraham Lincoln and the Emancipation Proclamation

"Excellent start, everyone," Mr. C concludes. "Tomorrow I'll come around and you can talk to me about your ideas and plans. Great thinking today!"

Teacher Reflection

"If you tell a group of 12- to 13-year-old kids they're going to learn about World War I and they're going to love it, you can almost hear their eyes roll. Building backward, using Understanding by Design (UBD), the final products were exactly what I had envisioned. I wanted them to have a finished journal written from the perspective of an American soldier. So I had to go backward and help them be able to do that. We didn't have a really good grasp on dramatizing history. I thought if I focused on dramatizing history, it would give us a better understanding of things that happened—even if we were fictionalizing. Kids need to see the story behind the facts of history. If you can get them hooked on the story, you've got them!"

—Chad Cooper

Transforming Literacy Teaching in the Era of Higher Standards © 2015 by Midge Madden and Valarie Lee, Scholastic Teaching Resources

Side-by-Side Lesson Analysis

Framework Element	Introduction to the Causes of World War I	➤ Teaching Moves	➤ Dramatizing History
Knowledge Production	Students read and gather information from multiple websites. They try to synthesize what they learn from websites with various degrees of success.	Provide scaffolding to students who need help in reading and determining key ideas from multiple websites. Model before students work on their own.	Teacher provides model clip (*War Horse*) and helps students unpack its creation. Students focus on one event and research information, using small-group collaboration for comprehension, writing, and performance.
Engagement	Students show enthusiasm and curiosity regarding Internet research. Students get frustrated when little explanation is given regarding the assignment.	Assess individual needs and provide support (model, note-taking sheet, summary frames). Assign groups so that stronger readers and writers are paired with struggling students. Build ways that all students can be successful.	Lesson is framed as an inquiry. Students are excited about their project, as evidenced by response to video clip, questions, and enthusiasm when choosing historical events to dramatize.
Independence	Teacher assigns work that must follow specific guidelines. Teacher allows too much independence and not enough direction in some situations.	Shift more responsibility to students; provide choice so they can make decisions.	Students are encouraged and trusted to be thinkers. Students are supported in their independence (through the worksheet, model video clip, and being given the time to ask questions to understand the project fully).
Voice	Students write group summaries with little opportunity for individual voices to be heard. Teacher gives limited student choice in the event to research and how to present it to an audience.	Find ways to share learning beyond the classroom.	Students exercise choice in topic for research and format of performance. Students perform dramatizations for other classes.

Mentoring Writers:
Do Students Have Good Models for Writing?

The first lesson, Taking Sides in an Argument, is a teacher-directed lesson. The second lesson, Side-by-Side Writing an Argument, incorporates key instructional shifts such as regular practice with complex text and reading and writing from evidence. Through the reading of mentor texts, students find voice in their own writing.

Teacher-Directed Lesson:
Taking Sides in an Argument

When students enter Ms. Sanford's room, they notice two large, bright yellow dots on opposite ends of the classroom. One is labeled "Yes" and the other "No." As they jostle one another to take their seats, Ms. S directs them to the question of the day on the board:

- Have you ever been in an argument?

Hands shoot up throughout the classroom. Marci replies, "All the time, especially with my little sister." After a few exchanges, Ms. S puts up the next question:

- What can you do to convince someone that your opinion is right?

Frank replies, "Tell them your point of view and give good examples so they will believe you." Ms. S nods. "Good. Today we are going to be writing persuasive essays, but before we do, I want to show you that it's not just important to have your own points in an argument but to also listen to someone with different ideas. This is so you can refute them, or prove them wrong. Now, everybody stand up!"

The students rise to their feet, laughing in anticipation. Ms. S explains that she will be putting a statement up on the interactive whiteboard. Students who agree should move to the "Yes" side of the room; those who disagree should move to the "No" side. "The key is, be prepared to say why and listen to people who disagree with you! Here's the statement:"

All students at our school should be required to wear a school uniform.

A near stampede takes place of students moving to the "No" side, but five students stand rather reluctantly on the "Yes" side. Ms. S asks the students who disagree to go first, and they start to give reasons, which she records on a T-chart on the interactive whiteboard:

- No, because every kid should be able to dress to show who they are.

- No, because clothes are really important to some people.

- I don't think so because there's no problem right now. Why change it?

Ms. S finishes the list of reasons and then turns to the "Yes" students for their reasons. She also records these on the T-chart:

- Well, maybe it might help cut down on kids who are bullied because their clothes are no good.

- Yeah, and it would be cheaper, too, because you wouldn't have to keep up with the latest styles.

Ms. S tells the class, "These are all great main ideas you could use to argue for or against school uniforms in a persuasive essay. But you also have to be prepared to address what the other side is saying. Can I have a volunteer from each side step forward?" Amanda and Louis step forward, and Ms. S instructs Amanda to read a "No" main point. Then she asks Louis to think of a way to argue against it.

> Amanda: No, because every kid should be able to dress to
> show who they are.

> Louis: But they can still dress the way they want outside
> of school.

Ms. S records this answer and then asks one more pair to come up and repeat the process. She then asks the students to sit down and they groan—they seem to have thoroughly enjoyed the debate. She hands each student a persuasive essay template to help them outline their thesis, three main ideas, and supporting points, as well as one main idea made by the other side. She then instructs the students to write as much as they can on their persuasive essay. She shows them a four-point rubric to guide their work. Students write for the next 15 minutes as Ms. S helps some of the struggling writers get started.

HOW DOES THE LESSON MEET THE STANDARDS?

Ms. S's students were clearly engaged in the argument activity. They enjoyed getting up and moving to different sides and arguing for their side. Ms. S also emphasized listening to another's argument, which is a critical part of the listening standards.

 ## WHAT'S MISSING?

Ms. S's lesson relies heavily on formulaic writing-to-a-prompt with no student choice in topic selection. Because students have already talked extensively about the main points and reasons, their paragraphs and essays end up being almost identical. Students do not get much actual instruction in writing an argument, rather the teacher gives a single scaffold of a template to all of the students, all but ensuring a formulaic essay. Other than the example oral argument, students have no model for how writers craft a persuasive piece.

PLACING STUDENTS AT THE CORE OF A STANDARDS-BASED LESSON

As you read the next lesson, consider how Mr. Raudenbush:

- integrates reading and writing together

- engages students in deep study of a mentor text

- uses authentic text to serve as an important model for students' arguments

- supports students as they find their voice and build confidence as writers

 Transforming Literacy Teaching in the Era of Higher Standards © 2015 by Midge Madden and Valarie Lee, Scholastic Teaching Resources

Student-Centered Lesson:
Side-by-Side Writing an Argument

Day One

As Mr. Raudenbush's students settle in, they quickly read the essential question for the day:

- What brings you joy?

Students quickly brainstorm and generate a personal list of answers in their writer's notebooks. Mr. R invites each of them to share one example and then tells them, "You probably won't be surprised to hear that I find reading very joyful! I know, I know. How can reading be a joy? Well, I don't think I would have a hard time arguing that it is because I feel passionate about it. I'm sure there are things on your list that you feel the same way about."

Mr. R then projects Mitch Albom's essay "The Joys of Summer" on the screen using the document camera. In the essay, Albom makes the case for kids doing nothing in the summer. Mr. R engages the students in an initial reading of the text, "Give the piece a first read and then turn and talk about the following with a partner: What were you thinking as you read 'The Joys of Summer' the first time through?" After a brief discussion, students do a second read, this time annotating the text, noting new thoughts, and then sharing their annotations with a partner. To check for understanding, Mr. R has the partners share with the whole class.

For guided practice, Mr. R models how to find an important line in the text and explain why it is important. He types his responses into a chart while thinking aloud for students.

Important Line From the Text	Why Is the Line Important?
I feel sorry for today's kids.	The writer is saying that there is something awful about the way modern kids spend summer vacation.

After completing another line in the chart together as a class, Mr. R instructs the students to read independently and continue to chart key lines and explain their importance. As he walks around, he gathers powerful examples to refer to later in the whole-class debriefing.

Mr. R then turns the students' attention to drawing conclusions about the text: "Based on the evidence in the piece, what is Albom's claim? What sentence in the text do you think best expresses the author's claim? Talk to your partner."

Susan and Francine turn immediately to the text and the important lines they noticed in their chart.

Francine: Well, I think it's this line [pointing to her chart]: "I can make the case for doing nothing all summer," because he comes right out and says it. Almost seems like he's saying it to us.

Susan: So, like, a "case" is a point he's trying to make. Is that the same as a "claim?"

When Susan and Francine share this, most of their classmates agree that this is the claim the author is making. Mr. R closes the first part of the lesson and mentions that the next day they will expand on what they've learned about comprehending the claims and finding support in the text to actually noticing the writer's craft.

Day Two

As students open their writer's notebooks, Mr. R reminds them, "Susan and Francine made a great point yesterday about the author stating his claim explicitly to the reader and how he references making a case. What I would like to do now is work more on what else we notice the writer is doing."

Students look back in their notebooks at their important lines chart to notice the craft of the writer. One section the students selected from the Albom essay was the six-sentence first paragraph:

> *Go ahead, kids. Lie in the grass. Study the clouds.*
> *Daydream. Be lazy. You have our permission.*

 Transforming Literacy Teaching in the Era of Higher Standards © 2015 by Midge Madden and Valarie Lee, Scholastic Teaching Resources

Several students note the short sentences in a row, such as "Lie in the grass" and "Study the clouds," while Nadia notices the one-word sentence "Daydream" and wonders aloud, "Is that a sentence?" Mr. R draws their attention to the comma in the imperative sentence "Go ahead, kids."

As they continue, Max notices that the author speaks directly to the reader ("you") and from the point of view of the adults. Mr. R responds, "Max, that gives me some great ideas for how I am going to emulate the writer in the first part of my piece. When I think of something joyful, I think of reading, so I am going to make the case for reading. OK, I want you to watch me." He takes a chair next to his computer, positioned so students can see the screen, and begins to draft. Students watch the screen as he starts, stops, goes back, and talks about his process.

The Joys of Summer	The Joys of Reading
Go ahead, kids. Lie in the grass. Study the clouds. Daydream. Be lazy. You have our permission.	Let's do it, folks. Flop on the couch. Let loose your imagination. Relax. Dive in. You deserve it.

Mr. R asks students to help him draft the next section of the piece, using the side-by-side technique. Students give suggestions that he often incorporates, but also sometimes changes, modeling the process of a writer incorporating feedback. Mr. R continues the emulation process by skipping to the last paragraph to write with his students. This "side-by-side" emulation of the mentor text process continues for ten minutes.

At this point, students have a model for the beginning and end of the essay. Mr. R then gives students the rest of the class time to develop the topics they brainstormed earlier. Francine continues emulating Albom through her entire piece. Josie's middle section bears little resemblance to the structure of the model. Jonathan decides to change the last paragraph instead of using the structure that was modeled.

Mr. R encourages each student to find his or her unique voice and supports students who find emulating the model frees them to write. He walks around reading over students' shoulders and writes down great sentences he sees that he can share, periodically announcing, "Hey everyone, look up here for a second. If you are stuck on this, take a look at this example and see if it helps you." Mr. R is pleased to notice that most of the students have successfully found their own voice.

Teacher Reflection

"As a writer, when you have a problem to solve, look at authors who had a similar problem to solve. Try it their way. Learn from them, incorporate what works, and add what you can come up with to make it better. Writing in front of students calls on teachers putting themselves out there as writers.

"If you can teach students problem solving, you are giving them something they can apply to any situation. They can internalize and transfer this skill to standardized prompts. It becomes their writing voice. 'This is not how I need to write for this test. This is how I write.' Read, notice, analyze, and talk about . . . then internalize and transfer . . . it becomes their writing voice but it takes time. One of my struggling students told me, 'I can write because I imitate.'"

—Dave Raudenbush

Transforming Literacy Teaching in the Era of Higher Standards © 2015 by Midge Madden and Valarie Lee, Scholastic Teaching Resources

Side-by-Side Lesson Analysis

Framework Element	Taking Sides in an Argument	➡ Teaching Moves	➡ Side-by-Side Writing an Argument
Knowledge Production	Teacher provides a pre-determined persuasive prompt, and, as a class, students come up with main ideas and supporting points.	Encourage students to notice elements of argument and writer's craft through modeling and gradual release.	Students learn how to structure language by noticing writer's craft as readers and by emulating it as writers.
Engagement	Students are engaged in oral argument, but the act of writing is limited.	Model good writing craft. Put up a student example as soon as possible. When students see that a peer can do it, they relax into it a little bit more.	Students have accountability, knowing "others will read my work."
Independence	Limited opportunities are provided for students to build independence in writing.	Do not assume students will be able to transfer oral arguments to writing an argument. Instead, provide modeling and gradual release to independence.	Students display a high level of writing output and claim ownership of their pieces.
Voice	Teacher gives students their own voice as they argue, but no choice in the topic for their arguments.	Provide a scaffold (emulating a model text) on which students can build their writing, allowing them to discover their own voice.	Students' voice eventually emerges through emulation and practice. Shared examples from student writing builds confidence and keeps the writing moving.

Chapter 4

Inquiry and Technology

"When I decide to teach fewer things, I actually teach more. Rather than lining up lessons as though they're floats in a parade, I find one clear focus and then attach a variety of skills and texts to it. . . . Going deep on a project actually means students wind up with a breadth of learning that the parade never would have accomplished."

—Sarah Brown Wessling,
2010 National Teacher of the Year

Today's teaching encourages teachers to move toward the background and release an increased amount of responsibility for learning to the students. . As teachers work collaboratively with one another to create units of study in and across grade levels, they must develop essential questions around which these units are framed and use backward planning to determine how students will showcase their knowledge. What will products look like? How will they be assessed? And students must have shared responsibility in this planning. Consequently, inquiry and digital skills become highly important as teachers understand how they are woven throughout our new standards. Realizing the goal—helping students become literate, productive citizens in the 21st century—demands sophisticated understanding of essential questions, inquiry, collaboration, and then sharing findings through technology.

According to Thom Markham, a psychologist, educator, and president of GlobalRedesigns, "The internationally benchmarked standards emphasize creativity, collaboration, critical thinking, presentation and demonstration, problem solving, research and inquiry, and career readiness" (Markham, 2012).

Linda Darling Hammond argues in *Powerful Learning* (2008) that teaching Common Core standards must include critical, creative, innovative, and inquiry-based thinking skills. She argues that research shows groups out-perform individuals in learning tasks and that project-based curriculums with an emphasis on technology have resulted in gains on standardized tests. Hammond also asserts that project-based inquiry learning can result in changes in motivation, attitude, and skills—including work habits, critical-thinking skills, and problem-solving abilities. The lessons in this chapter demonstrate the power and possibilities of inquiry-based teaching and learning and suggest ways that technology can support such practice. Each lesson has inquiry as its main focus and is infused with technology in some way. We look first at two lessons that focus on learning Greek myths and allusions in modern-day conversation and texts. The second set of lessons looks at ways teachers might reshape teaching the elements of fiction into inquiry and digital lessons.

Establishing a Purpose: Do Students Understand Why They Are Learning This?

The first lesson, Looking for Allusions in Popular Culture, is a teacher-directed lesson. The second lesson, Allusions and Their Importance in Today's World, incorporates key instructional shifts such as regular practice with complex text and building knowledge through content-rich nonfiction, including digital text.

Teacher-Directed Lesson:
Looking for Allusions in Popular Culture

Students file into language arts class, laughing and high-spirited. Ms. Damminger stands poised at the interactive whiteboard in the front of the room, ready to begin. She smiles, saying, "Get settled quickly, everyone. We've got a lot to do today!" Students quickly take their seats, in desks arranged in pairs, around the room. "What're we doing today, Ms. Damminger?" Kyle asks.

"You'll see, Kyle," Ms. D responds. "We're actually going on an 'allusion hunt.' But right now, sign in on your laptops and look at the PowerPoint I emailed you last night." Students spend several minutes reading the slides. Then Ms. D continues, "Now watch this clip closely." She plays an excerpt from the movie *Remember the Titans*. When it has finished, she asks, "Can anyone connect the title and this clip with something we've learned from reading different Greek myths?"

Rosie volunteers, "I know, it's *Remember the Titans*, a football movie. Matt adds, "Yeah, and it's awesome! I never thought about the title. The Titans is the name of the football team . . ." Kyle interrupts, "But weren't the Titans the original gods?" Ms. D nods encouragingly. "Go on, Kyle." "Well, I mean, maybe because the Titans in the movies were the first ever team to have blacks and whites play together and, you know, they were bigger and stronger and faster?"

"You got it!" responds Ms. D. "Now here's another one." She plays a segment from a song: *Achilles Heel*. "Any ideas?" she challenges. Rosie waves her hand. "Oh yeah, I know. The Greek hero, Achilles, had one weak spot; the lyrics talk about 'you are my weakness.' So, I guess an Achilles' heel is a weakness."

"Right again," nods Ms. D. "One final example, 'Stop being a such a jabberjay.'"

"Oh, easy!" exclaims the class. "*Hunger Games*!" "Right," says Ms. D. "But what's the allusion?" "Stop copying, don't be a copycat," responds Rosie.

"Oh, I get it now," murmurs Mario. "I think I know what to look for. Let's go!" Ms. D smiles. "Just a minute, Mario. Listen for the directions." She then explains that students will work in pairs to research, create, and share a presentation about Greek myths and modern-day allusions. Each pair will be given a myth and a vocabulary word or common phrase. They will also write

Transforming Literacy Teaching in the Era of Higher Standards © 2015 by Midge Madden and Valarie Lee, Scholastic Teaching Resources

a brief summary of their assigned myth. She pulls up the following research questions on the interactive whiteboard:

- What Greek myth did your word or common phrase originate from?

- How is this word or phrase used in our everyday language?

- What is an example of this use appearing in popular culture?

"Working in pairs, your task is to persuade an audience that allusions matter. How you do this is up to you: You can draw a free map, create a PowerPoint, or plan a performance, recorded on video or done live. We'll begin today, and have the next class period to finish and present."

Many students already know their myth and move right to their vocabulary word, searching for an allusion. Ms. D. cautions them, saying, "You'll need to slow down. I also want you to summarize the myth first."

"Aw, if we know the myth, why do we have to write a summary?" Josh asks. Ms. D responds, "That's part of the assignment. It will help you defend your allusion choice."

Students work intently during the 40-minute period. Ms. D moves about the classroom, stopping where students have questions. Three girls who received *fates* as their word are initially confused. Realizing that the Fates don't come from one singular myth, they struggle. "You can choose one myth or several," she tells the girls. "Just be sure your examples and your vocabulary word go together." The girls talk quietly. One offers, "Well, I remember a part from *Macbeth* and there's an allusion to the Fates there. Let's check that out."

As they do a Web search for "Macbeth and Fates allusions," conversations continue across the classroom. Pierce wonders, "Hey, there's this dartboard company called *Arachniad*. Let's figure out that allusion."

Peter and Josh connect an allusion to the Harry Potter series and disappearing water to the myth about Tantalus, a man tormented by the gods with insatiable thirst that cannot be quenched.

Most students accept their assigned vocabulary term; however, Kyle and Matt are dissatisfied. "*Hypnosis* is too easy," complains Matt. "Can we choose another?" Ms. D agrees, and they select *Amazons*. Kyle comments that the Amazons were "weird" because they were women who were really big, strong fighters. "Hmmm . . ." Ms. D murmurs, then moves on, suggesting they continue to read and think about possible allusions.

The end-of-class bell rings, and students look up. "Already?" they cry. Ms. D quickly reminds students that they will have another day to finish up. Students pack up and exit. Matt and Scott continue to talk about the project as they leave.

"I still don't get why we're doing this," admits Scott. Matt shrugs, then says, "Because we have to! But I guess it's supposed to help us in high school or something."

Teacher Reflection

"My teaching is different now in terms of the texts that I use and my expectations of students. Now that I know the research, this activity will be easier. As a teacher I need to understand the implications of who gets what term and myth. I had UBD training and addressed this brief research project with that in mind. I know the Common Core asks students to read, do mini-inquiry projects, and to use technology. This is what I had in mind when creating the lesson."

—Kara Damminger

HOW DOES THE LESSON MEET THE STANDARDS?

Ms. D has created an inquiry lesson that uses technology. She provides students with some choice in presentation style. Ms. D also clearly addresses both the speaking and research/inquiry standards. Students must develop a question, research it, and then share their project in a public forum (e.g., their classroom). They seem to be comfortable with the inquiry directive: "Here's the Internet; go search." Students have little difficulty navigating Web pages and finding everyday allusions. Ms. D also uses excellent exemplars (the *Remember the Titans* clip and "jabberjay" from *The Hunger Games*) to show that allusions are everywhere.

Her lesson/project allows for differentiation by assigning myths and vocabulary words based on difficulty and story complexity. She also monitors students' understanding well. In sum, the lesson is an activity to familiarize students with use of modern-day allusions. It presents good, engaging activities that use digital tools and some student choice to motivate. Students have fun as they connect modern-day terms to ancient Greek stories.

WHAT'S MISSING?

Matt's final comment suggests the central element missing in Ms. D's lesson: Students need to know why they are learning about allusions. Questions that resonate at the lesson's end are: Do students understand why they are hunting for allusions? Do they know why allusions matter in today's world? Because the lesson does not provide these answers, it is somewhat disconnected and fragmented and becomes simply a list of activities. Students haven't been given the idea that understanding allusions can help them get at the deeper meaning of a text.

PLACING STUDENTS AT THE CORE OF A STANDARDS-BASED LESSON

As you read the next lesson, consider how Ms. Johnson:

- pushes students to answer the essential question, "Why are allusions important?"

- invites students to map out their own projects

- provides class supports that allow students to be resources for one another

- sets up the first lesson to be an introduction to a more sophisticated understanding of allusion

Student-Centered Lesson:
Allusions and Their Importance in Today's World

"OK, students," Ms. Johnson announces, "here's the essential question for today's class: 'Why do allusions matter in today's world?'"

She reminds students that they have been identifying allusions in various texts—their literature anthology, newspapers, and advertisements in popular magazines. She continues, "I've been thinking of a good way to help us answer this and found some great ideas on the *New York Times* website—specifically, an article by Elizabeth Samet. "But first, who can define *allusion* for us so we all have a common understanding?"

Harold volunteers, "Well, we looked it up in our group yesterday." He reads from his notes: *a brief, usually indirect, reference to another place, event, or to words spoken by or that depict a person or fictional character.*

"Hmmm," responds Ms. J. "That's pretty fancy-sounding. Can you or anyone else put that in ordinary language? Maybe give us an example?"

Several students wave their hands, but Harold continues, "I can. I mean an allusion is just something that refers back to something else in another text or piece of literature. You know, if you call someone a 'Romeo' it means he's a great lover!"

The class laughs and Harold bows.

"Good!" Ms. J joins in the laughter. "Anyone have another allusion?"

Other students share examples, such as calling someone an "Edward" or a "Jacob" (references to the *Twilight* series), opening Pandora's Box, and the movie *Remember the Titans*. Ms. J asks if there are any more examples or questions about the definition of allusions. Then she challenges, "Does anyone know why it's important to identify allusions when you're reading?"

A few students shake their heads. Jerry offers, "Maybe so we know old words and phrases are important?"

 Transforming Literacy Teaching in the Era of Higher Standards © 2015 by Midge Madden and Valarie Lee, Scholastic Teaching Resources

"You're thinking, Jerry," Ms. J says, smiling, "but not quite. Anybody else? No? OK, then, let's return to today's question: *Why do allusions matter in today's world?* I'm going to give you the entire period to work on answering it—either individually or in groups. As you're doing this, also be thinking of the pros and cons of making allusions."

Ms. J passes out an essay titled "Grand Allusion" by Elizabeth D. Samet and displays the link on the interactive whiteboard for those who wish to read it online. "You might want to read through the entire essay first," she suggests. "Then go back and begin to hunt for allusions. Use highlighters or some other code to mark ones you know, the ones you find meanings to on the Internet, and the ones you find meanings to from someplace else—another person, a book, or even a guess." She pauses, then asks, "Any questions? OK, then let's get started. If you get stuck, ask me or others for help."

Several groups form immediately, students clustering in a corner or pushing desks together.

"Let's read the whole thing first," Zoey suggests to her group of three. Other groups decide to do the same, and the room grows quiet as students read Samet's essay. After ten minutes, Ms. J interrupts, reminding students to begin talking about the essay and looking for allusions.

"Even if you don't understand everything, talking to one another will help clarify the ideas," she says. She observes groups working and stops to offer suggestions or answer questions as needed. She reminds students to mark allusions and note how they know the history of each allusion. Jared's group motions to Ms. J, wondering how to find the meaning of an allusion if they can't find it in a Web search. "Well, you could ask others, look in a book, or maybe just try to guess for now."

"Aw, come on, Ms. J, can't you just tell us?" pleads Jared. "Oh, come on yourself, Jared," Ms. J quips. "If I tell you, how is that helping you problem solve or think?" "Yeah, I know." Jared smiles. "We can figure it out. Or at least we can figure out the allusions even if we don't know where they all came from."

Forty minutes pass with students sharing ideas, arguing about meaning, and racing to see who can find an allusion's meaning first on their computer's search engine. "Time's up," calls Ms. J. "Let's see how we're thinking. I have the essay up here on the interactive whiteboard. I want one person from each group to come up and circle all the allusions that they found." Once this is completed, Ms. J tells everyone to look at their notes to see what they might have missed. Included are

- I was reminded that each unhappy allusion is unhappy in its own way.

  — Leo Tolstoy

- Scylla of the swindle to the Charybdis of condescension.

  —Greek Mythology

"Nice work, class," Ms. J comments. "You've done the first part—finding some allusions. But more difficult is getting to the meaning behind them and using that to help you understand the essay's message. What did you find out?" Students volunteer the origin of each of the identified allusions and how they figured them out. Most were found on the Internet. "That was pretty easy," announces Zoey. "With a computer you can search for the answer to almost anything."

"Yeah, our group got all of them," adds Jared.

"Well, you're right in a way," agrees Ms. J. "With technology, it is easy to find out what an allusions means or refers to. But what about the 'so what' question? Why is knowing allusions important? I've highlighted some lines in the essay that may help your thinking. Talk in your groups to come up with a response."

Ms. J shows the following excerpt from Samet's essay:

Wimsatt and Beardsley's warning that identifying an allusion does not amount to the same thing as understanding its significance has renewed urgency in the current age of allusion—automation, for if the Web makes it that much easier for the allusion-hunter to bag his quarry, it does not necessarily tell him how to dress it.

Reading the excerpt, Jerry looks puzzled. "'Bag his quarry? Dress it?' I know this isn't an allusion but I don't get it."

"Guess you don't hunt," laughs Jared. "You bag your quarry when you shoot what you're hunting. You dress it when you skin it and make it ready to cook."

"Go on," encourages Ms. J. "You got the literal meaning; now how does it apply to allusions?" Now Jared looks perplexed. "Don't know, Ms. J," he says shaking his head.

Sarah, who hasn't yet said a word, suddenly exclaims, "Oh I get it! I think the writer's saying that it's not enough to just know the allusion, but you have to understand what it means. Then, you can really get what she's trying to say."

Ms. J grins. "You're almost there, Sarah. So what is the point of this essay?" "Knowing what allusions mean helps you get the writer's message!" Sarah proudly announces.

"Yeah," adds Jerry. "And if you don't know, you'll miss a lot of the writer's meaning!"

Side-by-Side Lesson Analysis

Framework Element	Looking for Allusions in Popular Culture	➤ Teaching Moves ➤	Allusions and Their Importance in Today's World
Knowledge Production	Teacher co-constructs knowledge of Greek myths and allusions with students. Previous discussions of myths aid in finding allusions and ascertaining their meaning.	Center activity around an essential question that gets at the importance of allusions.	Students co-construct knowledge of allusions to answer essential questions with a clear focus on the essential question of why allusions matter.
Engagement	There is a high degree of student engagement and interest in the project, although there is also student uncertainty as to why allusions matter in today's world.	Structure the research project as an inquiry. Model a close reading of a text where understanding of allusions is critical to comprehension. Have students read multiple texts doing the same.	Increased student expectations and responsibility result in a high degree of student-driven engagement.
Independence	Students have some independence as they work with partners to find modern-day allusions and relate them to the selected myth.	Encourage students to draw conclusions about the importance of allusions.	Students work collaboratively to understand the importance of allusions. The teacher intervenes only when needed.
Voice	Students have choice of working partner and presentation style.	Use an open inquiry format where students decide how to show their understanding of allusion.	Lesson begins around a central text but moves into student inquiry. Students interpret the text using digital tools and other sources. Students control the inquiry, seeking to answer the essential question: *Why do allusions matter in today's world?*

 Transforming Literacy Teaching in the Era of Higher Standards © 2015 by Midge Madden and Valarie Lee, Scholastic Teaching Resources

Amplifying Student Work: How Can They Share Their Ideas With a Wider Audience?

The first lesson, Annotating and Literary Analysis, is a teacher-directed lesson. The second lesson, Digital Annotating and Collaborative, Digital Literary Analysis, incorporates key instructional shifts such as regular practice with complex text and building knowledge through content-rich nonfiction. Furthermore, the lesson focuses on student choice and engagement as students amplify their work to a larger audience.

Teacher-Directed Lesson: Annotating and Literary Analysis

The students in Ms. Williams third period English class are attempting to answer one of the essential questions that frames their literature units:

- What is the relationship among the elements of a story?

Ms. Pridgen, the language arts supervisor for the middle school, is sitting in today to observe Ms. W's lesson. She notices right away that the students are comfortable with the task of annotating a text. Ms. W has taught her students different tools and symbols they can use to annotate their thinking on any text. Although these are posted on a chart in the classroom, Ms. P sees students annotating without referencing the chart—evidence that they have internalized this strategy.

Ms. W reminds her students that as they reread O. Henry's short story "After Twenty Years," they will need to consider how different story elements (symbols, conflict, characters) are connected. She challenges them to continue to go deeper in their annotations, looking for relationships in the story elements.

After ten minutes of independent reading, rereading, and annotating, Ms. W creates groups of four students and has them bring their annotated text and a writing utensil to these new groups. Ms. P notes that the students move quickly into these groups, possible evidence that small-group discussions occur regularly in this classroom.

"OK, everyone," Ms. W begins. "You have done a lot of work using the symbols to annotate the text and you have started to go beyond just identifying story elements to making connections between the conflicts. Your next task is to work as a group to create a graphic organizer that demonstrates your group's understanding of the multiple conflicts within the story." Ms. W holds up several examples of graphic organizers to remind students of the purpose: to graphically display an understanding of a complex concept.

As Ms. W talks, Ms. P hears her remind students to include in their organizer the relevant characters/entities with each conflict, the subject of the conflicts, and the type of conflicts. They also must use evidence from the text to support their thinking. "Remember, you already have good information in your annotated texts so be sure to refer to them as you cite evidence," Ms. W adds.

As she circulates around the room, Ms. P notices that most of the students are actively engaged in the discussion and are attempting to agree on some connections between the conflicts. She stops at one group and listens in as Ms. W provides some feedback. "I see that you've made a huge discovery that I was really hoping for. You created a place in the middle of the diagram for 'theme,' which means you really understand the interconnectedness of the story elements." Could you tell me more about the theme?"

Transforming Literacy Teaching in the Era of Higher Standards © 2015 by Midge Madden and Valarie Lee, Scholastic Teaching Resources

Tina explains, "Well, every time we added a new conflict, we kept coming back to this one idea: So, like, what do you do when you have to go against a friend?" Carlos agrees, "Yeah, so we thought that the connection might be that while friendship is really emphasized, it also seems that loyalty to a friend can only go so far sometimes!"

Teacher Reflection

"As Language Arts Supervisor, I've been observing teachers trying to move to Common Core lessons. One in particular comes to mind, where the teacher did three things especially well: called upon students to do close, critical reading for the purpose of making connections and analyzing a text; provided a method to promote close, critical reading (annotating the text, selecting symbols); and had students working in collaborative groups as well as writing for more than one purpose. I think one of the big moments in the lesson was when one group made a huge discovery that I was really hoping for: they found a place in the middle of the diagram for 'theme,' which means they understood the interconnectedness of the elements. Common Core calls on kids to examine the evidence and problem solve, even be creative as long as they can justify their work with evidence from the text."

—Amy Pridgen

✔ HOW DOES THE LESSON MEET THE STANDARDS?

Common Core calls on students to examine the evidence and problem solve; they can be creative as long as they can justify their work with evidence from the text. Ms. W provides opportunities for students to create their own graphic representation of the connections in conflicts from their group's collaboration. Examining how story elements work together is one of the reading literature standards. Several groups are able to make the connection between multiple conflicts and a central theme.

🔍 WHAT'S MISSING?

Students often view this type of work as solely contained within the confines of the English classroom and fail to grasp the greater implications and authentic connections to their own lives. Students need more opportunities to "learn how to learn" (Hammond & Barron, 2008) with tools and collaboration. Ms. W could capitalize on these tools to enable her students to share their thinking with a larger, authentic audience.

🎓 PLACING STUDENTS AT THE CORE OF A STANDARDS-BASED LESSON

As you read the next lesson, consider how Mr. Raines:

- uses technology to extend students' annotations to a larger audience

- encourages students to use digital tools to collaborate

- gives students a voice in the class

- suggests ways students can expand their knowledge through deeper inquiry with a variety of partners

Transforming Literacy Teaching in the Era of Higher Standards © 2015 by Midge Madden and Valarie Lee, Scholastic Teaching Resources

Student-Centered Lesson: Digital Annotating and Collaborative, Digital Literary Analysis

Mr. Raines' middle school students have been working with digital text-marking, or annotating, of literary texts, specifically short stories, to help them better understand the themes of friendship and loyalty. Students have also been talking about texts and learning the ways that different responses to a piece of literature can enhance and deepen interpretation of that text.

For the current lesson, Mr. R is expanding students' annotating and discussions from simply face-to-face in the classroom to the virtual world. He has created a collaborative weblog with another middle school teacher, Ms. Franz, and her students in California. Two students from Mr. R's class and two from Ms. F's class will share their digital annotating with each other. The students are familiar with the use of document tracking and commenting. They can use digital tools to underline, highlight, and insert comments on a piece of text.

Mr. R begins the lesson by reminding students that group comments can push face-to-face partners to go deeper in examining the interrelationship between the elements of the story. Listening to everyone's ideas can help students answer the essential questions:

- How do the characters' actions impact conflicts?

- What is the significance of the identified conflicts?

- How do these conflicts relate to our themes of friendship and loyalty?

Then he springs the surprise on his students. "Exciting news, everyone! We're going to partner with students in Palo Alto, California!"

"Awesome!" several boys exclaim. "Can we go there too?"

Mr. R laughs. "You guys take everything too far! But yes we can go there too—virtually!"

"Awww, not the same, Mr. R!" they respond.

Mr. R. nods sympathetically and smiles. "Yeah, I know. Life is tough! But seriously, you are all pretty good with digital tools, and this will give you a chance to be heard outside of our classroom. We're going to blog!"

"Huh? How are we going to do that?" Sam asks.

"Well, I've set up a weblog and paired you. Ms. Franz has done the same with her students in Palo Alto. Four of you will read the same short story and comment as a kind of 'group think' blogging project."

"That's cool," several students say as they high-five.

"But there are some rules. Just like we have to respect one another in our class, online there are digital citizenship guidelines. I'm putting them up here. Take some time to read through them."

Mr. R provides a few minutes for students to read. "Any questions?" he asks. "OK, good. Just be sure you follow these whenever you write blog posts."

Then he continues, "Once you get online, type in the weblog address I've put up on our whiteboard. I've also posted your partners' names in Palo Alto and the short story that all four of you will read. Everyone still with me?"

Heads nod; some students put their thumb up.

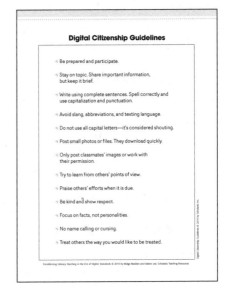

Digital Citizenship Guidelines— downloadable pdf is available online (see page 16)

Transforming Literacy Teaching in the Era of Higher Standards © 2015 by Midge Madden and Valarie Lee, Scholastic Teaching Resources

"OK, great. First introduce yourself to your Palo Alto partners. This will be your first blog post. Then scroll down the blog to where you see the link to your short story. I've pasted the story link right in the blog. Click on the link and pull up your short story text. It will be a pdf so you can use the comment tools to annotate right on the digital text."

Mr. R pauses and waits for everyone to sign in to the blog.

"OK, ready?" he asks. Observing that all have successfully signed on to the weblog, he continues. "We're going to do something called annotexting. It's just like annotating, except when annotating you work on paper and are usually alone. Annotexting is cool because you can put down your thoughts and reactions to something you're reading using different Web tools. You can collaborate with people not in our classroom."

Owen jumps in, "Yeah, way cool! I can see how California kids think about the same story, right?"

"Absolutely." Mr. R nods. "Once you annotate your copy of the document, save your notes as a hyperlink into the blog. After everyone in your group has put up an annotated text, you can read one anothers' comments. Remember, as you look at your partner's annotexting, think about how it is shaping your own thinking. Perhaps someone else's thinking causes another question to emerge. Or maybe it causes you to reread a section with new ideas or a new focus."

After two rounds of collaborating through shared documents, several students notice that besides annotexting indicating deeper thinking about the text, many of the comments and insertions the groups add focus on personal experiences. Renee notices that her group's comments all seem to keep circling back to the theme of loyalty.

Mr. R asks, "You've all done well reading this closely and carefully; what I am noticing is that you keep connecting to your own experiences. Maybe we can chart some questions that might be worthy of further exploration." He writes the following questions on the whiteboard:

- Are certain friendships more worth fighting for than others?

- Does loyalty only go so far, no matter how good a friend might be?

- Is extreme loyalty to another person only asking for trouble?

"So, we have some really interesting questions here that you could pursue and find out more about. But what could we do with the information?" Mr. R asks.

One student offers, "It might be interesting to read something more modern and see if we can compare them. Friendship and loyalty across both. Like two different stories."

Another student suggests, "What about looking for examples in society? Is there a problem with friendship and being loyal?"

Mr. R and the students decide that they would like to continue their learning by getting perspectives on these topics from students outside the United States. "Maybe they don't view friendship and loyalty like we do," Manny points out during the discussion. The students and Mr. R decide to pursue an inquiry project with students their age but in another country. Mr. R is already thinking of using websites such as ePals and Around the World in 80 Classrooms that provide teachers with opportunities to connect with classrooms around the world in order to work on a common project. His students' successful foray into digital amplification and collaboration encourages him to keep stretching beyond the walls of his classroom and school.

Side-by-Side Lesson Analysis

Framework Element	Annotating and Literary Analysis →	Teaching Moves →	Digital Annotating, and Collaborative, Digital Literary Analysis
Knowledge Production	Requires students to understand and address the standards of the lesson.	Show students how to use digital tools and digital citizenship to construct knowledge.	Students use annotexting to work collaboratively with others to build knowledge about interrelationship among the elements of the story.
Engagement	Students work in collaborative groups and address the speaking and listening standards.	Introduce digital tools, such as annotexting, which will allow students to interact with text in new ways.	Students are engaged with one another and their online peers in an authentic task. Using technology also heightens interest and collaboration.
Independence	Students use annotating to work toward greater independence with comprehending complex texts.	Scaffold the use of collaboration tools and work with students to model how to deepen their thinking.	Students use collaboration tools to deepen their understanding of theme and other literary elements in literature.
Voice	Students have choice in how to organize their thinking graphically.	Introduce the use of digital editing tools to use for annotexting.	Annotexting allows digital documents to be shared nationally or globally. Students have voice in how to broaden the inquiry.

Chapter 5

Re-envisioning Teaching and Learning

It's first period in Edison Middle School, and there is an air of excited anticipation in the classroom. Students push desks together to make an amphitheater formation. Two boys carry a table to the front of the room, then hoist two chairs and an armchair over Leila's head to place beside it.

"What are you doing?" Leila asks. "You almost knocked me over!"

"Sorry, Leila," apologizes Larry. "Gotta get the stage set before Ms. DeGarmo gets here!"

Leila shakes her head and laughs. She gathers up the props—a copy of *The Wave*, two glasses and a pitcher of water, a microphone—and carefully places them on the table. Then she stands back, hands on hips, eyes scanning the front of the room.

"It's good, Leila," Demond observes from the back of the room. "Looks pretty close to an *Oprah* set. For a classroom, anyway. Where's Ms. DeGarmo?"

"Hey guys," Ms. D says as she enters the room. "This looks great! You've got the whole thing set up! Are we ready?"

Twenty students resound in chorus, "Yes!" And from the back of the room, James adds, "Yeah, videocam all set up and microphone turned on, so sound system's working."

Ms. D sits in the newly constructed amphitheater, settling in as part of the audience. She gives a slight nod to Shanai to begin.

"Well, welcome, everyone, to *The Oprah Show*!" Shanai (playing Oprah) smiles and saunters to the table, sitting in the armchair beside the table. "We have an exciting show today about a strange phenomenon called 'the Wave.' Are you ready?"

"Yes!" shouts the audience.

"OK, then. Let's give Robert a round of applause." Shanai greets Jordan (playing Robert) and shakes hands. "Welcome Robert, nice to have you on the show. What brought you here today?"

Head bowed and hands clasped, Robert begins softly, "I need to tell my story. Because of the things I've been through, I have changed. I was the class loser, not like I didn't know that. The things kids said about me. . . . I may not be a genius but I'm not stupid! Before 'the Wave,' girls ran away from me. I think they could use my scent as an insect repellent!"

Oprah murmurs, "I'm sorry, Robert. But what about your family? You have a brother, right?"

Robert jerks his head up angrily. "Yeah, I have a brother! All my life I've been compared to him, and I'm sick of everyone talking about that. Jeff this, Jeff that. I'm not him! Being in someone's shadow is not that great. 'The Wave' gave me a chance to be someone. I got swept up like everyone else . . . the idea of being equal, not Robert the Loser."

Oprah offers Robert a drink of water. He takes a sip, then continues. "I was accepted! It boosted my ego, I'm not going to lie. I was given a second chance and I wasn't going to let anyone come in between me and that chance. I was devastated when I found out it was all a lie. I never saw it coming, that's for sure. I remember crying really hard for what I had lost, for what I had gained. It was kind of like being left in a bit of limbo. I didn't know what I was going to do, but most of all I was terrified I'd have to go back to being Robert, to being lonely. I don't want to be alone."

Oprah sighs. "Thank you, Robert. We don't want you to be alone so I hope things work out for you." She claps, inviting the audience to do so as well. Robert stands, gives a soft "Thank you" and leaves the stage.

The next guest, Josh (playing Ben Ross), enters and is welcomed by Oprah. "Now we'll hear from Mr. Ben Ross, teacher and the person who started 'the Wave.' Welcome, Ben. What do you have to say for yourself?"

Ben turns his hands up in a gesture of apology. He begins, "'The Wave' started out as a classroom experiment but in fact it turned out to be something more. I came up with an idea of how kids could work together in a group, and I soon felt like I was part of it, too, with Robert becoming my bodyguard. Then I realized it was turning into something terrible. When David and Laurie came to my house it made me come to my senses. I had to show students that sometimes the popular thing wasn't always the right thing. I heard my students chanting against those not in 'the Wave.' I told my students we had to stop; they were becoming little Nazis. I knew some would be upset, but my decision was made."

Ben pauses and stares into the audience. "That's all I can say," he murmurs. "And I'm sorry."

"Well, thank you, Ben," Oprah responds. Clapping, she watches Ben leave, then announces, "Now we have our final guests, two members of 'the Wave,' Laurie Saunders and David Connors. So, Laurie and David, can you help us understand this Wave? How did it happen?" She addresses Kiera (playing Laurie Saunders) and Trevor (playing David Conners).

"Well," Laurie begins, "it all started in Ben Ross' history class. We'd watched a video on the Holocaust, and all found it pretty upsetting; couldn't understand how the Germans could just sit there and act like they didn't know the Nazis just slaughtered people. So Mr. Ross had us begin a student group. We called it 'the Wave,' and it was supposed to help us understand how people cannot see the truth."

David chimes in, "Yeah, and I was overzealous with 'the Wave.' Even had an idea to make it work for the football team. I even broke up with Laurie. I remember her saying, 'You're so idealistic, David.' Which I kind of am." [laughing]

Laurie interrupts, "To make a long story short, 'the Wave' started out fine but then got bigger and bigger. I told David a million times, it's wrong, it's wrong. He didn't listen. Everyone wasn't allowed to be in 'the Wave.' It wasn't equal."

David nods. "I know, I know. I was caught up in it. When I pushed Laurie to the ground, I was sad and sorry. I suddenly didn't want to be in 'the Wave.' That's when we went to Mr. Ross and created a plan to end it."

Laurie and David smile at each other, quietly holding hands. Oprah jumps up, thanking both and clapping vigorously. " Well, thanks to these two young people, 'the Wave' phenomenon has ended, and it sounds as if everyone involved has learned a lot from the experience. Thank you all for joining us today on *The Oprah Show*!"

Reflections on Transformed Practice

Inspired by Todd Strasser's novel *The Wave,* and provided with choice and independence, the students in this middle school classroom, we can see, are totally engaged in an activity that transformed into an "Oprah Show." Although *The Wave* was a required novel in the language arts curriculum, Ms. DeGarmo completely changed the way she had traditionally taught the book, inviting students to make decisions and assume responsibility for their learning. Discussing themes and analyzing characters is not new to the teaching of novels; however, working collaboratively in small groups, searching for textual evidence to build a portrait of a character, writing a script for that character, and finally becoming that character in a student-chosen exhibition of knowledge is new.

Students' and teachers' comments made after watching the *Oprah* performances help us further understand the power of such student-initiated learning.

"I love how the characters came alive."

"It's clear that the message of *The Wave*—a school experiment gone awry—was deeply ingrained in your students."

"I felt for Robert; I know what it's like to be invisible."

Ms. D also expressed surprise mixed with proud emotions at her students' accomplishments. "You know, they told me creating these character portraits was 'making it real'—those were their words. And they had fun with it. The students in the dramatization felt it helped them understand the characters and the book as a whole. It was very multilayered; kids had to do character analysis, infer, and then decide moves to create dramatic performances. I see potential for teachers to be able to adapt a lot, try different angles. It was awesome to see how my kids interacted across different groups, almost as if the characters were talking to one another. The collaborative script writing worked well, too. When I asked if my students wanted to create more character portraits and performances, they gave a resounding 'Yes!'"

Concluding Thoughts

If we revisit our framework, "Students at the Core: Knowledge Production, Engagement, Independence, and Voice" (see page 11), this project addresses each component. Creating scripts and character performances for Strasser's *The Wave* caught students' attention; it was fun and they became highly engaged as they read, wrote, listened to one another, and gave spoken, dramatic performances. For this language arts class, the character-portrait project provided a perfect vehicle for the integration of the standards in a student-centered classroom.

The portrait of this middle school classroom demonstrates the possibilities of text dramatizations, but it also serves as a call to educators to think differently about teaching and learning as they address new, higher standards. If schools' goals are to help young people become successful contributors to society in the 21st-century (the CCSS graduate profile), students must be critical thinkers, problem solvers, collaborators, communicators, and reflective learners (Partnership for 21st Century Skills, 2011)—ideas that align perfectly with the goals of the Common Core and other modern standards. But more important, students must be at the center of learning. It is their dreams and their visions that must be held dear as they—children growing to young adults—inhabit our schools.

Schools, and the teachers and administrators that shape them, face multiple challenges in today's world of rapid, exponential change. If we consider the explosion of knowledge over the past years—between 1999 and 2003 more new knowledge was created in the world than in the entire history of the world preceding (Hammond, 2013, p. 14)—the dilemma of how to conceive of school curriculums becomes evident.

As we alluded to in the introduction, the Common Core State Standards are not meant to be a national curriculum. The standards are the overarching ideas that can serve as guides in our teaching. Teachers and administrators must be careful not to "standardize" the Common Core or any similar standards by limiting teaching possibilities to only that which is explicitly mentioned.

Many of the lessons we present in our book place students at the center of learning. Students need to see that learning matters. They need opportunities to try out independent thinking and to "talk back" to content and curriculum. Without their "buy in" and curiosity about ideas, schools will remain places where teachers give assignments and students simply follow along. This certainly doesn't mean that today's teachers should eschew planning and instruction, only that it must look different. Hammond (2013) explains the difference in 21st-century learning requires students to:

> Be able to learn to learn. To understand core ideas as well, with the capacity to un-assemble new information, analyze, synthesize, and evaluate which leads to credibility and utility of that information. Facts need to be carefully chosen to build a schema in a field of work. Kids need to learn to learn which changes the way we think about curriculum. The way in which we have to think about knowledge is understood in a different way today.

As knowledge shifts and grows, so should programs and curriculums. Educators, such as the ones featured in this book, grapple with critical questions every day, including:

- What should be included in units of study?

- How can we write curriculum that spans kindergarten to grade 12?

- What strategies can help manage new kinds of classrooms and new assessments to measure this new way of learning?

To answer these, teachers must strive to truly understand the needs of their students, changing programs and curriculum as indicated by those needs. They must look more closely at students' individual strengths and talents and the kinds of supports needed to ensure successful learning. Wiener (2013) says it well: "Yes, we need challenging twenty-first century curriculum for all students, but saying that all students need the same curriculum is not realistic."

Re-envisioned schools embrace the idea that there is a rigor to learning. Today's standards indeed "up" the rigor. But many teachers hesitate. A comment we hear over and over illustrates much current thinking: "I keep hearing a lot about rigor and building stamina, but I have students who can't handle the work I give now. What happens when I increase the difficulty?" And we counter with: "Is it that they can't do it, or that we *believe* they can't do it?"

We argue that the Common Core has the potential to turn teaching upside down, to move out of the traditional classroom and into student-centered learning spaces. However, teachers need support and the permission to teach in new ways. The stakes are higher than ever for teachers to "get it right." But if we are to get it "right"—truly reconceptualize schools for the 21st century—teachers and administrators must experiment with new ideas and new ways of teaching, especially since there is no one way of "getting it right."

The Common Core extends a hand and simultaneously throws down the gauntlet. There is no going back, only moving forward. By doing so, we can become the very best teachers, and our students can become the very best at whatever they choose to pursue. This will happen if we always remain true to our beliefs about teaching, learning, and, most important, our students.

> "... the only way to do great work is to love what you do. If you haven't found it yet, keep looking. Don't settle. As with all matters of the heart, you'll know when you find it. And, like any great relationship, it just gets better and better as the years roll on. So keep looking until you find it. Don't settle."
>
> —Steve Jobs

Notes

Transforming Literacy Teaching in the Era of Higher Standards © 2015 by Midge Madden and Valarie Lee, Scholastic Teaching Resources

References

Professional Resources Cited

ACT, Inc. (2006). *Reading between the lines: What the ACT reveals about college readiness in reading.* Iowa City, IA: Author.

Adams, M. J. (2009). The challenge of advanced texts: The interdependence of reading and learning. In E. H. Hiebert (Ed.), *Reading more, reading better: Are American students reading enough of the right stuff?* (pp. 163–189). New York: Guilford.

Britton, J. (1970). *Language and learning.* Coral Gables, FL: University of Miami Press.

Calkins, L. (2010). *Launch an intermediate Writing Workshop: Getting started with units of study for teaching writing, grades 3–5.* Portsmouth, NH: Heinemann.

Calkins, L., Ehrenworth, M., & Lehman, C. (2012). *Pathways to the common core.* New York: Heinemann.

Common Core State Standards for English Language Arts and Literacy in History/Social Studies, Science, and Technical Subjects. (n.d.). Appendix A. Retrieved October 27, 2014 from http://www.corestandards.org/assets/Appendix_A.pdf

Common Core State Standards Initiative. (2014). English language arts standards introduction: Students who are college and career ready in reading, writing, speaking, listening, & language. Retrieved October 27, 2014 from http://www.corestandards.org/ELA-Literacy/introduction/students-who-are-college-and-career-ready-in-reading-writing-speaking-listening-language/

Fisher, D. & Frey, N. (2012). *Text complexity: Raising rigor in reading.* Newark, DE: International Reading Association.

Hammond, L. D. & Barron, B. (2008, October 8). Powerful learning: Studies show deep understanding derives from collaborative methods. *Edutopia.* Retrieved October 27, 2014, from http://www.edutopia.org/inquiry-project-learning-research

Hammond, L. D. (2013, June 5) *Teaching for deeper learning: Developing a thinking pedagogy.* Keynote speech at the 2013 Redesigning Pedagogy Conference. Reprinted in *Rethinking educational paradigms: Moving from good to great.* CJ Koh Professorial Lecture Series No. 5. Office of Education Research, National Institute of Education, NIE/NTU, Singapore.

International Reading Association. (n.d.). *Literacy implementation guidance for the ELA Common Core State Standards* [White paper]. Retrieved October 27, 2014, from http://www.reading.org/Libraries/association-documents/ira_ccss_guidelines.pdf

Markham, T. (2012, February 21). Project-based learning and Common Core Standards. The Whole Child Blog. Retrieved October 27, 2014, from http://whatworks. wholechildeducation.org/blog/project-based-learning-and-common-core-standards

National Governors Association Center for Best Practices & Council of Chief State School Officers. (2010). Common Core State Standards for English language arts and literacy in history/social studies, science, and technical subjects. Washington, DC: Author.

Partnership for 21st Century Skills. (2011). Framework for 21st Century Skills. Retrieved October 27, 2014, from http://www.p21.org/our-work/p21-framework

Shanahan, T. (2012, November 21). Pre-reading and ELLs: Let's take off the training wheels. Shanahan on Literacy. Retrieved October 27, 2014, from http://www. shanahanonliteracy.com/2012/11/prereading-and-ells-lets-take-off.html

Shanahan, T. (2011, August, 21). Rejecting instructional level theory. Shanahan on Literacy. Retrieved October 27, 2014, from http://www.shanahanonliteracy. com/2011/08/rejecting-instructional-level-theory.html

Thomas, L. (2013, May 1). The "monster" at the end of the Common Core. *Education Week*. Retrieved October 27, 2014, from http://www.edweek.org/tm/articles/2013/05/01/ fp_thomas_commoncore.html

Wiener, L. (2013, July 13). Comment in S. Sawchuk, NEA delegates endorse Common-Core supports, but not testing. *Education Week*. Retrieved October 27, 2014, from http://blogs.edweek.org/edweek/teacherbeat/2013/07/nea_delegates_endorse_ common-core-.html

Wessling, S. B. (2013, February 17). Does the Common Core demoralize teachers? *The Huffington Post*. Retrieved November 3, 2014, from http://www.huffingtonpost.com/ sarah-brown-wessling/common-core_b_2702209.html

Literature Cited

Albom, M. (2011, August 7). The joys of summer. *Parade Magazine*. Retrieved October 27, 2014, from http://parade.condenast.com/122204/mitchalbom/110807-the-joys-of-summer/

Bloor, E. (1997). *Tangerine*. New York: Scholastic.

Popov, N. (1998). *Why?* New York: North South Books.

Samet, E. D. (2012, February 3). Grand allusion. Retrieved October 27, 2014, from (http://www.nytimes.com/2012/02/05/books/review/grand-allusion.html

Strasser, T. (1981). *The Wave*. New York: Laurel Leaf.

Yolen, J. (1988). *The Devil's Arithmetic*. New York: Penguin Books.